Patricia H. Hinchey

Becoming a
CRITICAL EDUCATOR

DEFINING A CLASSROOM IDENTITY, DESIGNING A CRITICAL PEDAGOGY

PETER LANG
New York • Washington, D.C./Baltimore • Bern
Frankfurt am Main • Berlin • Brussels • Vienna • Oxford

Library of Congress Cataloging-in-Publication Data

Hinchey, Patricia H.
Becoming a critical educator: defining a classroom identity,
designing a critical pedagogy / Patricia H. Hinchey.
p. cm. — (Counterpoints; vol. 224)
Includes bibliographical references and index.
1. Critical pedagogy—United States. 2. Politics and education—United States.
I. Title. II. Counterpoints (New York, N.Y.) v. 224.
LC196.5.U6 H56   370.11'5—dc21   2002034024
ISBN 0-8204-6149-0
ISSN 1058-1634

Die Deutsche Bibliothek-CIP-Einheitsaufnahme

Hinchey, Patricia H.:
Becoming a critical educator: defining a classroom identity,
designing a critical pedagogy / Patricia H. Hinchey
–New York; Washington, D.C./Baltimore; Bern; Frankfurt am Main;
Berlin; Brussels; Vienna; Oxford: Lang.
(Counterpoints; Vol. 224)
ISBN 0-8204-6149-0

Cover design by Dutton & Sherman Design

The paper in this book meets the guidelines for permanence and durability
of the Committee on Production Guidelines for Book Longevity
of the Council of Library Resources.

© 2004 Peter Lang Publishing, Inc., New York
275 Seventh Avenue, 28th Floor, New York, NY 10001
www.peterlangusa.com

Printed in the United States of America

To Miss Hinchey and the 28 most excellent fifth-grade students
who consumed her intellect—and heart—
during the 2003–2004 school year.

And also to Elizabeth, Miss Hinchey's unofficial aide
and indefatigable supporter.

Contents

PART II
CONSIDERING DESTINATIONS: TRUTH,
CONSEQUENCES, AND THE CRITICAL VISION

Foreword

To understand why I—someone unknown to anyone in the field of educational theory—should be writing a foreword to a book on critical educational practice, and why anything I might have to say might matter, you need to know two things about me. First, I am a new teacher, with a summer's worth of education courses and two months' classroom experience in a school populated by "at-risk" children; and second, I am the daughter of the author—which is to say, I am a twenty-something, White female who enjoyed a comfortable, middle-class upbringing (perhaps some of you will identify?) and who has been around the author as this book was evolving.

When the early chapters were being written, occasionally a draft would turn up in my email with a note saying, "I think you may find this interesting." At the time, I was working in the juvenile division of the Legal Aid Society in New York City, and so of course I was interested in Chapter Three, which described conditions I knew many of my clients experienced. By last summer, although I'd left Legal Aid and had not yet entered the classroom, I still found a draft of Chapter Four interesting because I already understood how the policies of self-interested politicians had affected, for example, all of the homeless children I'd known. But last weekend, when I was reading drafts of Chapters Five and Six after teaching for two months, I turned to my mother and said, "You know, before I was interested to read this stuff. Now, I find it so painful I can barely stand it. Now, every paragraph brings the face of a particular child to my mind and I can't stand what I see happening to them."

And that was when I was asked to write this Foreword—because my teaching experience has put a human face on the theoretical material that follows. Already, I know which of my students—all of whom might be described as "other people's children"—have been summarily dismissed as inevitable failures by school authorities; already, too, I know how unique and precious each of my students actually is, no matter what others may think of them; and already I see how important it is for smart and courageous people to enter teaching and to fight for better conditions for these students and countless others like them in cities, in rural areas, on reservations—wherever poverty and an uncaring society threaten their futures.

The interest I felt before I was in a classroom has been turned to passion by coming to know my students as the wonderful people they truly are. My hope here is to share my understanding and that passion with you before you take up the rest of the book, so that your reading can be informed, as mine was only recently, by the constant presence of real children who desperately need the kind of teacher this book hopes to educate and inspire.

I write, then, to introduce you to my class. While of course I've changed names and left out many of the more painful facts of their daily lives in order to protect their privacy, I hope to give you a sense of both their unique potential and the incredible challenges they face.

Damon has big, brown eyes that sparkle with more mischief, more intelligence, and more confidence than any child I've ever known. During the first days of class, he was quiet and cooperative. Yet, when an administrator came into my classroom on the third day of school to scan my class list and offer anecdotes about some students, she immediately asked about Damon's behavior and warned me that he'd had many problems with teachers in the past. When I remarked on his good behavior and said how much I enjoyed his sense of humor and sharp wit, her skepticism was obvious. I soon noticed that if Damon's name came up when I chatted with seasoned teachers in my school, they consistently responded with "Ohh . . . that kid," or "Ohh . . . him." It's been obvious to me from the start that Damon is indelibly labeled as a hopeless troublemaker. When I eventually asked for advice from a mentor on how I might best maintain a productive relationship with him, I was told that I can't "save them all," and that I should simply try to help him pass fifth grade, so he can move on from us and become the problem of his middle school.

Not surprisingly I suppose, soon after our pleasant first days together, Damon and I were at war. He was making disparaging comments under his breath, distracting the other students, and undermining my authority. I was constantly singling him out and yelling at him; when I tried to call his mother at home one night, Damon hung up on me twice. Things improved only after I stopped invoking home and school authorities and tried a principle promoted in this text: I started treating Damon with more respect and talking to him about respectful relationships in general. After some weeks, we are now on much better terms. We have very real conversations about his life and his future, even though Damon makes it clear that he doesn't entirely trust me. I sense that he wants to, but many adults have disappointed him, and he refuses to let me hurt him. Yet, little by little, I chip away at his hard façade.

One day, he proclaimed to me that he hates teachers. Refusing to allow him to get away with this blanket statement, I probed as to why he hates teachers. He eventually disclosed pieces of his very tragic, very disheartening educational history, a long string of incidents demonstrating that whenever anything bad happens, accusing fingers point first and always at him. I don't know which parts of Damon's story are true, and which parts he has rewritten in his own mind. To be honest, I don't care. If Damon committed the acts that he was accused of, I believe that he was acting out a self-fulfilling prophecy. He has repeatedly been told that he is a troublemaker who can't do anything right. He has listened to numerous adults tell him that he will never make anything of his life. He knows that the school has given up on him. And so, he acts accordingly.

In poor urban settings, parents, teachers, and other people who are emotionally invested in, and connected to, school age youngsters speak of losing these adolescents to the streets. Well, I refuse to lose Damon to the streets. I see worlds of potential in his eyes, and I believe that this child can, and will fulfill, all of his dreams. One day, I told him that he is very charismatic. Unfamiliar with the word, Damon looked up "charisma" in the dictionary. We talked about what it meant, and the next day I overheard Damon explaining the word charisma to another student and bragging that I described him as charismatic. My hope is that Damon realizes that I believe in him, and that he will find the strength in my support to do fabulous things with his life.

Brianna, I've learned, comes from a troubled home. When she came to school very upset one day about an incident there, another teacher notified Children's Services. As a result, Brianna was called out of my class repeatedly throughout the day to speak with assorted officials. When she came back into the classroom at the end of the day with a single tear trickling down her face, I had time only to quickly ask her, "Brianna, honey, are you okay?" She clearly was not okay, but said she was, so I continued performing the one million tasks that teachers must complete at the end of the day.

A few moments after my conversation with Brianna, I watched as Damon approached her to ask what was wrong; Brianna shared with him the details of her clearly traumatic experience. The interaction that I witnessed between these two young people stopped my heart, and made my own eyes swell with tears. Damon responded to Brianna's worries with more grace, more maturity, and more empathy than I was able to muster when speaking with her that day. He listened to her sad tale, absorbed her fears, and then assured her that she could talk to him any time that she needed to. I was surprised not only by Damon's maturity, but by Brianna's willingness to confide in him. Even though I'd never seen any signs of a friendship between them, she obviously saw something in him that many adults in his life have not recognized—kindness, dignity, and maturity. No: I don't want Damon lost to the streets. And, I want to help create a safe space for Brianna.

I'm still trying to figure out what to do for Stacey. She and her mother arrived from a foreign country a few weeks before the school year began. Her father, her siblings, and her puppy had to remain behind, however, because her parents could not afford for the entire family to move to the United States. Stacey is very shy, and she rarely attempts to speak in class, although she does write in English—often about her father. She writes how much she misses him, how much she hopes that he'll be able to move to New York soon.

Stacey's mother waits for me almost every day after school to discuss Stacey's English language acquisition and progress in my class and to share her concern that her daughter is both falling behind in school and not making friends. So I've asked Mary, one of the most affable girls in my class, to keep an eye on Stacey, to make sure that she has someone to sit with at lunch. Mary does a good job of trying to include her as I've asked, but I frequently worry that Stacey feels incredibly lonely and isolated.

Now, Douglas is a genius. I'm sure of it. He is one of those students who constantly talks, doodles, and makes distorted, funny faces in class, but he can answer any question that I ask him, even when I am positive that he is not paying attention. Douglas solves math problems in under ten seconds. When he writes, he uses language beautifully, and he composes very thought-provoking pieces. He is also seriously hearing impaired. I wear a hearing device around my neck, and Douglas wears a hearing device in his ear so that he can hear me throughout the day. This device was not available to me for the first three weeks of school because an administrator placed it an "undisclosed location" and would not release it due to "personal reasons." Eventually the coordinator for all hearing impaired students in my region came to my school, went to the appropriate administrative office, and managed to move someone to locate the device. Now, Douglas can hear me. Still: it's too bad that although his body was present, he missed the first three weeks of school.

Kimberly comes from a very religious home, but her mother no longer lives there. Her father cares for and financially supports all eight of his children without any assistance. Kimberly is sweet and smart and motivated. She likes to assume "extra projects" and classroom responsibilities. When I teach, Kimberly takes copious notes and is usually the first student to volunteer to answer a question.

At the end of the first week of school, when it became evident to me that Kimberly had not yet brought in her school supplies, she asked me if she could have extra time to bring her supplies to school because her father could not afford to purchase school supplies for her and her siblings at the same time. When her eye glasses broke in class one day, Kimberly started to cry, telling me that her father would be so upset when he saw the glasses because he can't afford to buy her new ones. Kimberly adores her father and worries about him constantly. She brags daily that he was a general in a South American army. Asked to write about a special event, Kimberly wrote about her father's birthday. She always writes about her father. Perhaps it's her way of keeping her father close; perhaps she fears that like her mother, he will leave home too.

Michael is rambunctious and unruly and clever. He has a difficult time staying seated for long periods of time, so I frequently allow him to complete his class-work standing up, or at various locations around the classroom. Michael also wants to be right next to me *all* of the time. When the class meets on the carpet (as every elementary school class must do now in New York City), Michael always sits at my feet. He plays with my shoes, he grabs my arms, and he touches my hands while I am speaking. When I take the class to lunch or for a practice fire drill, Michael always maneuvers himself to the front of the line, right next to me. Everyday he begs me to allow him to eat his lunch with me.

Michael loves to talk to me. As the days go by, and he trusts me more, Michael provides me with more and more details about his life. He told me that his parents are divorced, and that his mother and siblings live in another state. Michael lives in New York City with his father, although he had wanted to stay with his mother. He writes about missing his friends and his sister and his hometown. I can't help wondering if his extreme attachment to me has something to do with his mother's absence.

I teach at an elementary school in New York City that has an extraordinarily high immigrant population. Many of my students are new to this country, and most of their parents speak little to no English. And, like many other immigrant communities around the country, the neighborhood in which my school is located is plagued by high rates of poverty, violence, and single parent households. Before I accepted this teaching position, I was cautioned that my biggest struggle would be dealing with the parents of my students. I was warned that these parents don't care about their children, and that they place no value on their children's education. I was cautioned that the parents of my students have no work ethic, and that they will be consistently confrontational when dealing with teachers and other school personnel.

And yet, on Meet the Teacher night, 20 out of 28 of my students' parents attended. They had many thoughtful, intelligent questions for me to answer—how will the new math curriculum prepare their children for the standardized tests that they must take in the spring? How will their children receive grammar instruction under the new workshop model of literacy that all New York City public schools were mandated to implement? How are the English language learners going to pass the mandatory standardized tests *and* keep up with the fifth grade curriculum? Many of these parents waited one hour to speak with me about specific concerns that they have regarding their children. These are parents who love their children every bit as much as parents of children who are lucky enough to attend well-funded, suburban schools. These are parents who worry as much about their children as my parents ever worried about me.

Like their parents, my students worry about issues that never crossed my mind as a child. They write about family members and close friends who have been killed by random or intentional gunfire in their neighborhoods. They write about divorce. They write about their desires to witness their mothers smile and laugh, and their wishes to help their families pay the bills. Lisa writes about memories of her deceased mother, generally joyous memories of parties and bedtime stories, although some refer to every child's darkest nightmares—being lost, crying out for a parent who isn't there, the fear of being left alone.

My students talk to me about fathers they have never met. They tell me when they are disappointed by loved ones who have broken promises—"My dad promised to take me to my brother's graduation from Army school, and he never called me." "My mom promised to throw me a birthday party, and then she forgot my birthday." They talk to me about apartments that are too small to hold them and their siblings. They tell me about their parents' addictions. They discuss broken hearts and fifth-grade drama. They probe for details of my life, and inquire as to the well-being of my dogs frequently.

My students also talk to me about their dreams. Francis wants to be a scientist and a doctor and a lawyer. Lawrence wants to be a professional wrestler. Michael wants to be professional baseball player and a teacher. Mary wants to be a pediatrician. Damon wants to be a rapper *and* graduate of Yale's law school. All of my students fantasize about earning enough money to help their mothers and fathers pay the bills. Bradley wants to hire his mother a housekeeper so that she doesn't have to clean their house after she comes home from work, exhausted. Kimberly wants to be a movie star who earns a lot of money so that she can help her father care for her and her siblings.

When my students discuss their dreams, it is difficult for me to conceal my anger. I am so incredibly angry that these children have already been dismissed by the educational system, by New York City, by this wondrous land of opportunity—the United States of America. My students come from families who left poverty-stricken countries to create a better life for their children. I become so angry when I think about the lives that these children will have after me. I look at their eager eyes, and I want to point them straight to the stars. I want to protect them from the world. I want to promise them moms and dads and college and good health and safety and any dream that their little hearts desire.

Before I began teaching I was warned that it would take up all of my time and energy. Well, no one sufficiently expresses the amount of time and energy. My students consume all of me—my time, my energy, my thoughts, my attention, and my dreams. I can't think of anything *but* them. I never expected to feel so emotionally consumed. I was also told that I would love the kids, but I didn't expect to love them as much as I do. Nobody told me that there would be moments with the students that are so sweet that my heart would literally ache for them.

They are the most special children . . . and they are the most typical children. They are like so many others facing the same disadvantages and dismal fates if teachers and others don't take very seriously the need to help change their futures.

I believe this book can help you understand why current unconscionable conditions exist and how you can help to change them. I hope that as you read, you keep Damon and Brianna, Stacey and Douglas, Kimberly and Michael, Lisa and Francis, Lawrence and Bradley in mind. Ultimately, I believe this book matters because *they* matter. They need you to read the following pages thoughtfully and consider joining the struggle to improve their lot. I hope you will.

Shawna Hinchey
New York City
October, 2003

Preface

When I think about current conditions for public education and about the task of educating teachers, a phrase I often use with my friends comes to mind: "I wish I had a magic wand." I tend to make that wish when I'd like to extricate good people from difficult circumstances, from complex messes not of their own making, from fates they don't deserve. I use it, too, when an overwhelming challenge presents itself and the immediate and impossible question seems "Where do we begin?"

These factors all describe precisely the conditions I see children, teachers, and my colleagues caught in. Social inequities continue to grow worse because as a society, we like to pretend that racism and other forms of discrimination are behind us; that American society genuinely offers equal opportunity to all its constituencies and is without social class distinctions; that any existing poverty is a result of laziness and lack of initiative. Meanwhile, corporations and politicians concerned with profit rather than people are increasingly promoting rhetoric and implementing policies to define and constrict the entire field of education—even as professional educators are being educated (or pummeled) into believing that political issues can be kept outside the classroom, that education can be a politically neutral process. The results of these many factors include an array of vicious contemporary conditions for children, teachers, and teacher educators.

Wanting to make a difference in these deplorable circumstances, and wishing for but lacking a magic wand to impose a quick fix, I've opted instead to try to pursue change beyond my own classroom with this text. The issues are complex: How to persuade readers that there is no such thing as apolitical education? That race, class, gender, sexual orientation matter very much indeed—and not just to students, but to teachers themselves? That the agenda being imposed is a deliberate one that has been crafted over recent decades and that serves not children but those who already wield great wealth and power in American society? That there are real alternatives to current trends and conditions—but that they will not be realized without the active engagement of teachers on behalf of the children they are ethically bound to represent?

My best attempts to answer those questions comprise the following pages, which I sincerely hope will persuade teachers of the need to become the "public intellectuals" Henry Giroux and others call for, and to accept responsibility for educational and social activism. Unless and until teachers become engaged in active struggle against current oppressive conditions, schools will continue to mass produce "human capital" for greedy corporations while simultaneously failing to meet the needs of children and helping to eliminate teaching as a profession—most especially, as a caring profession.

If only I had a magic wand and could spare us all the struggle.

I don't, and I can't.

Instead, I hope that this text persuades readers the *only* way out of this mess is to march straight through it, determined to make a difference, and that it will move them to join the march.

Acknowledgments

As always, I remain grateful to all those who have forced me to think—and then to think again: mentors, students, colleagues, writers, speakers, absurd as well as saintly administrators, friends, foes, and family. I am especially grateful to the many among you who have refrained from thrashing me the countless times in recent months I said, "Yes, sure, of course, I will . . . as soon as the book is finished."

Most specifically, I thank Jacqueline Edmondson, Rosa Roman Perez, and Melanie Morgon for careful reading and insightful critiques of drafts; also, Vicki Kay Carter and Gena Lengel for riding in on their white horses and carrying me forward as I dashed madly to the finish line.

Finally, I want to note my deep gratitude for Chris Myers' unwavering and invaluable encouragement and support. We who enjoy his good care of our work know how blessed we are.

Grateful acknowledgment is made to the following for permission to reprint previously published material:

Peggy Albers, "Praxis II and African American Teacher Candidates." Copyright 2002 by the National Council of Teachers of English.

Joel Spring, *The American School: 1642–1999.* Copyright 1996 by McGraw-Hill.

Margaret Chin & Katerine Newman, *High Stakes: Time Poverty, Testing and the Children of the Working Poor.* Working paper, 2002, Foundation for Child Development, New York City. Research generously supported by the Foundation for Child Development, the Ford Foundation, the National Science Foundation, and the MacArthur Foundation.

PART I

Beginning the Journey:
Thinking about Our Thinking

When I do not know myself, I cannot know who my students are. I will see them through a glass darkly, in the shadows of my unexamined life—and when I cannot see them clearly I cannot teach them well.

PARKER PALMER
"The Heart of a Teacher"

CHAPTER 1

Starting Points:
Assumptions and Alternatives

I think that it is a profoundly democratic thing to begin to learn to ask questions.

My dad's been dead a long time, but one piece of his advice still kicks in every time I get behind the wheel of a car: *Pat, never trust a blinker.* I never do. As a result (and unlike my husband), I have never found myself in the path of a car coming straight at me after failing to make the turn promised by its cheerily flashing—and lying— blinker. I'm still acting on Dad's instructions, though I don't generally get into the car chanting *Don't trust a blinker . . . Don't trust a blinker. . . .* Long ago I translated his principle into what is now my automatic behavior.

All of us move through every day exhibiting countless similar behaviors, habits we acquired from someone, somewhere, that now seem simply the best or right way to do something. Driving easily offers many more examples: Maybe we never exceed the speed limit, or routinely exceed it by five miles per hour. Maybe we never let the gas gauge fall below a half or quarter tank, or maybe we routinely wait until it falls to the E line.

What's interesting and important to notice about these habits—and what also has important implications for educators, as I'll explain shortly—is that they resulted from someone or other, at some time or other, making some assumptions, or holding some beliefs, or reaching some conclusions, about the nature of the driving experience. My dad assumed, for example, that other drivers are not trustworthy, and so he always drove defensively. Many people assume that all laws should be obeyed, to the letter, at all times, whether they deal with driving or stealing, and so they automatically obey the speed limit just as they automatically return lost wallets and tell the whole truth on their income tax returns. Other drivers assume that the police ticket only drivers exceeding the speed limit by more than five miles an hour, and so they speed by just that much. Still others assume that all automakers set the fuel gauge to register E long before a tank is actually perilously close to empty.

The point here is simple but essential: Our lives overflow with countless daily acts that are essentially habits, actions we take without thinking about them. We no longer question whether the assumptions underpinning them are sound—if, in fact, we ever did think about those assumptions when authorities like parents were schooling us in certain behaviors (like not trusting a blinker—certainly I never asked my dad for his evidence that other drivers were untrustworthy). And yet, unexamined assumptions are critical; they shape our behavior, and our behavior has consequences for ourselves and others.

For example, a driver who assumes that the speed limit is really five miles over the posted limit may be headed for an expensive encounter with a police officer; a driver who believes the E on a gas gauge meaningless may be in for a long walk. While we generally choose actions we believe are safe or productive, what we actually experience depends on whether the assumptions behind our actions are sound. My dad, an authority figure I never doubted, was usually right—but that's just my good luck. Other authority figures, including adults who insist that it's safe to speed moderately or that a car will never stop running until the gauge registers below empty, are often wrong.

It's essential, then, to take a conscious look at our assumptions because they largely determine the effectiveness of our strategies and the quality of our results: sound assumptions usually lead us to effective actions and satisfying results, whereas unsound ones more often prompt unwise actions and unhappy consequences. Driving habits are a simplistic example, but the principle is a sound one that applies to far more important examples. Most especially, assumptions about schools, students, teaching, and learning all influence teachers' actions—and teachers' actions have enormous consequences not only for the students whose future they shape, but also for the American society those students will eventually join as workers and democratic citizens. Most of us can afford a speeding ticket, but this text will argue that we can no longer afford schools peopled by educators who act without being conscious of their assumptions, their choices, and the likely consequences.

Why Theory and Philosophy Matter: From the Abstract to the Practical

Having themselves been students for at least eight to twelve years, and possibly sixteen years or more, most people have countless ideas about what constitutes the right or best things for teachers, students, and parents to do: Teachers should talk, and students should listen. Teachers should assign homework, and students should do it. Teachers should give tests and assign grades, and parents should accept the grades as good indicators of what a child is or is not learning. Teachers should tell parents what their children need to do, and parents should impose the teacher's strategies on their children.

Precisely because these routines have been part of American public education for so long, teachers might be hard pressed to explain the assumptions underpinning them, even though they've probably completed several courses on teaching and learning. It is not difficult, however, to discredit many assumptions once they are exposed. For example, once I was working with a group of student teachers who complained vehemently that their students would not do homework. In response, I asked why they were assigning homework—and they were, to a person, baffled by the question. *What do you mean?* they asked. *We have to give homework.* When I asked why again, the best they could come up with was *Because that's what teachers do* (Hinchey 1992).

As my own research has indicated, however, many widespread but unconscious assumptions about the need to assign homework can be identified: *assigning homework ensures that students get essential practice,* for example, or *assigning homework is an effective way to keep students, who have too much time on their hands, out of trouble after school.* Once exposed, many such assumptions are easily refuted with readily available, abundant evidence to the contrary. For example: simply assigning homework does not mean students will benefit from doing it (Strauss 2002). Common homework assignments often force students to practice a skill they have long-since mastered, as when senior high students are routinely required (as are third graders) to underline subjects and verbs or to circle adjectives in sentences; tasks like these are also time-wasters because they are not useful in life outside the classroom. Moreover, many students are already heavily scheduled with sports, church, work, parenting and other activities, so that their problem is too little discretionary time rather than too much. And, these examples merely scratch the surface of why there is often a great deal more sense in students' refusal to do nightly homework than in teachers' insistence on assigning it.

Despite the power of such faulty assumptions to shape classroom habits, and despite the frustration those ill-founded routines often produce, there are several reasons that practitioners rarely articulate and examine the unconscious ideas driving their practice. First, American schools have changed little in over a century (Cuban 1993), making for very long and very ingrained traditions. Second, teacher education courses focus most often not on the *whys* but on the *hows* of schooling: not on why to assign homework or to use multiple choice tests, but on how much homework to assign and on how to word a distractor on an exam. And, the *hows* are usually presented as prescriptions from educational researchers who have tried to attain the institutional status of natural scientists by conducting research in pursuit of definitive findings about what is called "best practice." As a result, much of their work reaches teachers in the form of authoritative directives to be followed, not ideas to be examined. The teacher is not to probe Bloom's Taxonomy for weaknesses, but to be sure that questions on an exam go beyond recall to other levels of cognitive skill; the teacher is not to question limitations of the Skinnerian principle of positive reinforcement, but to provide stickers to students who have spelled every word correctly.

And finally, even if teacher educators were inclined to ask students to examine the theory and assumptions underpinning practice (as they often are not), experience tells me that it is exceedingly difficult to get students to take theory and philosophy seriously (Hinchey 1992). As they approach the terrifying prospect of being alone in a classroom with thirty unpredictable young people, education students themselves generally demand recipes for what to do and scorn abstractions offered for thoughtful reflection.

The result is, naturally, a lot of people going through motions they do not fully understand and have never consciously chosen, a situation unlikely to produce results matching even the best and most earnest of good intentions. It is this situation that provides the impetus for this book, which asks readers to take time now, wherever they may be in their careers, to think through a variety of educational ideas that have startlingly different implications for classroom action. Our assumptions, beliefs, theories, and philosophies about schools and learning have a direct impact on how we conduct ourselves in classrooms, consciously or not; every action we take reflects some particular line of thinking and eliminates another at the same time. If we assume we have to assign homework, for example, then we won't have classrooms without it, whether it's effective or not.

Developing a Personal Stance

This being the case, I suggest that all educators need to start thinking much more consciously about classroom routines they've accepted as desirable or necessary without scrutinizing them, simply because they constitute "what teachers do." Given that assumptions produce behaviors and behaviors have consequences, educators need to make informed choices for themselves. Instead of passively accepting classroom advice and practices as revered hand-me-downs from teachers who have come before, or routinely assuming that distant experts like Bloom and Skinner always know better than a parent what a particular child may need, teachers need to think for themselves in terms of what to believe about, what to offer, and how to treat the children who actually populate their classrooms.

This text offers readers an opportunity to identify their own assumptions, to explore alternatives, and to make conscious choices about their own practice—although it does so in a context that unabashedly endorses the choices of the critical educator. Despite the philosophical orientation of this work, however, the choice of where to stand ultimately will be the reader's own. Perhaps even more important than which stance a reader chooses is the act of consciously choosing a stance, rather than mindlessly defaulting to one out of habit.

A first step toward careful reflection and choice is recognizing that consciously or not, anyone who has ideas about what schools "should" be or do is already aligned with one paradigm of education or another. Accordingly, the balance of this chapter will sketch two competing paradigms, providing a context for readers to begin reflecting on their own past and future alliances. Identifying an existing alliance is only a preliminary step, however. To begin evaluating their initial inclination, readers will need to understand the assumptions that undergird it—and that means, in turn, that they need to understand how particular kinds of life experiences shape the thinking of teachers and students alike. Chapter Two, therefore, focuses on teacher experience and thinking, while Chapter Three focuses on the life experiences of students who often come from very different backgrounds, and so experience the world very differently, than their teachers. Taken together, these three introductory chapters are intended not only to help readers become aware of the nature and sources of their thinking, but also to help them expand their thinking about teachers and students different from themselves.

In addition to better understanding and expanding their own thinking, readers working to choose consciously between paradigms need an in-depth understanding of how their objectives and consequences differ. Therefore, Chapters Four and Five offer a detailed look at the rhetoric and results of dominant educational rhetoric and policy, while Chapter Six offers a more detailed look at elements of the critical alternative sketched below. These last chapters will make clear that the choices teachers make between paradigms not only dictate very different behaviors on their part, but also promise dramatically different consequences for students as well as for the future of American democracy. For those who begin identifying themselves as critical educators, an appendix listing resources and allies provides an immediate bridge to next steps in developing a personal critical practice (or *praxis*—action based on conscious reflection).

Following below, then, are preliminary overviews of deeply rooted historical assumptions embedded in contemporary American educational practice as well as of critical theorists' starkly contrasting vision. Both sketches are necessarily oversimplified, intended to provide only a skeletal framework for the chapters that follow.

Historical Possibilities: Traditional Goals

The influence of historical thinking on contemporary education is strong, as recent legislation illustrates. As the twenty-first century opened, politicians of every persuasion took every opportunity to echo widespread voter dissatisfaction with public schools (Robelen 2000), and over time, standards and standardized testing emerged as popular responses to perceived problems with student achievement. That President George Bush succeeded in promoting legislation forcing each state to implement statewide testing (Robelon 2001) suggests that many people see little problem with the task of identifying what students should learn and then assessing their learning through standardized tests. Generally, the thinking behind such testing seems to be *We pretty much know what students need to know, and we know how to find out if they've learned it; we just need accountability to keep teachers and students on task in classrooms.* As is common in much public discourse, the assumptions behind this assertion are unarticulated (and unsupported).

However, any assertion about what students should learn in schools depends ultimately on the answers to other questions: *What, exactly, are schools for?* That is, what are they supposed to accomplish? For example, a school whose primary purpose is to prepare students for jobs immediately after graduation, as technical schools do, would define "what students need to know" very differently from a school whose primary purpose is to prepare them for application to Ivy League universities, for example, as Stuyvesant High School in New York City does. As this example demonstrates, there is (or should be) a direct link between a school's goals, or what it intends for students to be able to do or be, and its curriculum, or what information and practice students need to realize the school's goals.

The fact that politicians have imposed statewide testing despite the obvious diversity of individual public schools (where a single district may house separate vocational and academic high schools, or may have a concentration of English-speaking students in one elementary school and Spanish-speaking students in another) indicates an enormous assumption on their part: *however different individual schools and students may be, we can expect thousands of American schools to share some inherent crucial goal or goals that can be met if all students and teachers are forced to focus on a single core of information and skills.* What kind of goals could be so critical and so widespread as to justify statewide testing? What curriculum is likely to ensure that those goals are realized? The answers lie in historical conceptions of the purposes of public schools and traditional notions of curriculum.

Many people have heard the United States described, as it so often is, as a melting pot, but few are likely to have thought much about what that phrase signifies: gathering together a diverse group of individuals, applying a process intended to blend the individuals into one mass, and eventually producing a homogeneous standard product. Historically, and for clear political purposes, public schools have been responsible for the process of transforming individual students from a wide variety of backgrounds into some ideal *American*.

While the United States has always prided itself on welcoming immigrants, it has also historically preferred that immigrants be white, Anglo-Saxon and Protestant (WASP)—or, in the case of non-Protestants, Native Americans and other people of color, to immediately learn to look, sound, and behave as if they were WASPs. The country has never welcomed any cultural elements (language, for example) from those outside that mold, because the Founding Fathers placed all social, political and economic power into white, male, Anglo-Saxon Protestant hands. Not surprisingly, those hands have historically kept a firm grip on their power. In fact, the white, male elite specifically looked to the first government-sponsored schools, common schools, to ensure that the social structure and values they endorsed remained dominant. As increasing tensions developed between the Anglo-Saxon community and between immigrant Irish, enslaved and free African-Americans, and Native Americans, there was growing worry about the possibility of intermarriage and contamination of Anglo-Saxon blood and culture by "less civilized" others. The common school was intended to defend the theoretically superior Anglo culture from the influence of these others by educating the young as the Anglos thought desirable (Joel Spring 1997, 79). In this tradition, schools were expected to demonstrate to students the *American*—or right—way to think and act, erasing the traditions of their native cultures.

While the historical goal of producing a homogenous American citizen is certainly linked to bigotry, many offer a more defensible rationale for political purposes in schools, including efforts to promote an American identity among diverse student populations. For example, violence is common among disparate groups competing for survival in a new environment, and there are always such groups in American society; once they were Irish and Polish, and now they are perhaps Hmong or Palestinian, but immigrants are always with us. Many still believe that schools can reduce violence among ethnicities by encouraging immigrants to shed their old identities in favor of becoming *American*.

Moreover, no government can exist indefinitely without a loyal citizenry, and governments everywhere—in Japan and Germany and Saudi Arabia as well as the United States—have used schools to inculcate the young with political doctrine. All leaders, monarchists and socialists and democrats alike, want to stay in power and maintain political stability, and that is possible only if the young in every country grow up believing that their particular political system is the best possible political system. To that end, schools are expected to produce citizens who trust and support their government and its policies.

It is easy to see that such political purposes as cultivating a national identity and encouraging enthusiastic patriotism have produced many of the strongest traditions in American public schools. For example, teachers lead students daily in pledging allegiance to the flag, and every February profiles of national heroes George Washington and Abraham Lincoln mushroom in school windows nationwide. History books highlight military might and glory to stimulate pride, and simultaneously ignore the country's less glorious moments, like the genocide of Native Americans, to maintain trust in government authority. The curriculum becomes a list of sanitized and carefully selected facts that all Americans are supposed to know: *Who was the first president of the United States? When was the Declaration of Independence signed? What is the significance of December 7, 1941?* Political purposes, then, are always embedded in public schools and account to some degree for lawmakers' confidence that a one-size-fits-all curriculum and accountability system is feasible.

Closely related to the political goal of creating loyal citizens, and also essential to maintaining the country's status quo, is the economic goal of creating loyal capitalists. In the United States, democracy has become synonymous with capitalism, which schools are to promote as the American way. Essentially, schools are expected not only to extol the merits of capitalism, but also to produce hard workers and energetic consumers.

In practice, these goals shape the curriculum via exclusion: no criticism of capitalism is allowed in schools. Perhaps the strongest example of historic intolerance is an attack on a social studies textbook written by Harold Rugg, who was a professor at Columbia University when the controversy started in 1939.

Believing that schools should educate students to be intelligent and critical consumers, Rugg designed several lessons on those topics. His cautions to consumers inflamed the Advertising Federation of American, which issued a pamphlet titled "Facts You Should Know about Anti-Advertising Propaganda in School Textbooks." To support the charge that the textbook was anti-American (anti-capitalist) propaganda, the pamphlet cited an exchange between two men from Rugg's book in which one man dismissed advertising claims that a motor oil was superior, noting that when he personally tested the oil on copper, it proved corrosive (Spring 1996, 251). The combined efforts of the Federation, the Hearst newspapers, and B. C. Forbes himself reduced sales for Rugg's text from 289,000 in 1938 to 21,000 in 1944—and prompted the spectacle of the Binghamton, NY school board calling for the books to be burned (Spring 1996). The late 1990s demonstrated that the same spirit of censorship is functioning today, when school officials in Ridgewood, NJ, on three days' notice, canceled the performance of an original fourth-grade play critical of Nike and Disney's exploitation of Third World labor (Rana 1998).[1] As demonstrated here, critics of questionable business practices have been traditionally, and strenuously, excluded from American public schools.

Other elements of the economic agenda for schools are less explicit but nonetheless pervasive. If capitalism is to thrive, it must not only have workers, but it must have workers ready, willing, and able to do whatever work businesses need done. And, it needs a large pool of appropriately trained labor in order to keep wages down. When common schools were founded, the country was moving from an agrarian to an industrialized economy, and factories needed hordes of docile workers prepared to accept long hours of tedious labor. Rote and restrictive routines in the form of lining up, marching, and maintaining silence were considered beneficial training for the routines of factory life. Much of modern schooling comes from this tradition.

The authoritative teacher (like the factory supervisor) set tasks and determined how long the obedient students (like employees) worked at them. If students found every day filled with repetitive and boring labor, if their own interests and opinions were rigidly excluded from the classroom, and if they complained—well, what of it? Such was life, in schools and factories both, and students might as well get used to it. In fact, such *is* life in schools, which Bowles and Gintis have described—in their original 1976 text as well as subsequent editions through intervening decades—as "prepar[ing] people for adult work rules by socializing people to function well and without complaint in the hierarchical structure of the modern corporation" (1).

So pervasive and tenacious is the rhetoric exhorting students to prepare themselves for tedious and uninteresting work that many readers, no doubt, will hear their own parents and teachers echoed in common and apparently timeless injunctions: *Of course it's not fun, it's not supposed to be fun—learning is hard work. . . . I go to the office/plant/store and work and get paid in money; you go to school and work and get paid in grades. . . . The teacher isn't there to entertain you, s/he's there to teach you, so just do as you're told.* By the time students reached the factory (or the corporation), they were (or are) well-trained to quietly endure its tedious labor and authoritarianism.

The idea that schools should shape workers is also evident in the ubiquitous tracking system, where curricular options like the college preparatory track or the vocational track are designed to prepare students for the next step toward their work life, whatever it might be. Indeed, the schools' responsibility to prepare workers to fill labor needs of all kinds is so zealously embraced that it sometimes manifests itself even in the lowest grades of elementary school. I actually know a kindergarten teacher who, forced by administrative injunction in the late 1990s to design vocational education for five-year-olds, settled on having the children try on different hats. Of the school's many possible and historical purposes, preparing students for jobs is among the most entrenched. It would be no surprise, then, for both the twenty-first century lawmakers who mandated statewide testing and the state officials who designed those tests to simply take for granted that any state curriculum *will* include basic job training, however that might be defined.

Finally, schools have traditionally been expected to prepare students appropriately for social life in the democracy, adopting mainstream values that, again, keep daily life—and the status quo—humming: respect for authority, for example, and belief that hard work and education provide a sure route to success. The country needs citizens who can live together peacefully, who respect laws, who cause others no problems, and schools have a very long tradition of working to produce such citizens. According to Spring (1996), sociologist Edward Ross first conceived of education as serving a police function by inculcating values that had formerly been imposed by church and family; if schools could do a good enough job at what might be called character education, citizens would learn to police themselves (12). Schools, then, appeared to be potentially useful mechanisms for producing the kinds of people that certain elements of society deemed desirable.

Certain personal characteristics have always been hallmarks of Protestantism and what is thought of as "the American character": hard work, competitiveness, self-reliance, pursuit of wealth, respect for authority. While these may not appear on the official curriculum, much of school routine still certainly intends to instill these values—which, not coincidentally, also work to reinforce capitalism. If all it takes to succeed is hard work, for example, then anyone who is poor must be lazy—an idea that helps protect the economic status quo from criticism, despite some harsh social realities. In 1999, for example, nearly one-third of all children in the United States under age 18 were living in poverty (very conservatively defined), with nearly twelve percent of them experiencing moderate or severe hunger (Trends 2001).

The idea that schools can and should work to instill values that will keep American society healthy and happy explains why so many topics outside the traditional academic curriculum have been adopted by schools over the years: driver education, values clarification, sex education . . . any social imperative that arises. However, precisely because many social topics, especially as they relate to sex—AIDS, homosexuality, birth control—are highly controversial, state and local authorities face enormous challenges when specifying topics for official curricula. Often, such decisions are made in a heated, circus-like atmosphere that leaves communities deeply divided. This was the case in New York City when Chancellor Joseph Fernandez introduced the draft of his Rainbow Curriculum, a multicultural effort intended to alleviate ethnic strife, and lost not only the ensuing curricular battle but also his job. Fernandez was attacked and driven from office because a very few paragraphs in the plan's several hundred pages suggested that schools acknowledge homosexual families (Kelly 1993). Contemporary calls for a more liberal social agenda in schools have consistently been rabidly opposed by many who endorse the traditional, conservative mindset reflected in such curricular classics as *The Scarlet Letter*.

These, then, are the essential historical purposes of schools: the political, which ask schools to indoctrinate patriotic citizens; the economic, which ask schools to train compliant, productive workers and acquisitive consumers; and the social, which ask schools to nurture hardworking, self-reliant, law-abiding community members. In every instance, the intention is to preserve the American status quo. These ideas—these assumptions—about what schools should accomplish are so ingrained that they function today as taken-for-granted and self-evident facts, sufficiently ingrained to allow lawmakers to confidently impose state curricula and testing.

How these traditional political, economic and social goals are embedded in contemporary educational rhetoric and reform schemes will be detailed in Chapters Four and Five. However, this abbreviated sketch provides enough background for the reader to appreciate the stark contrasts of the alternative, critical vision of goals for schools which follows.

An Alternative Agenda: Critical Goals

Like traditionalists, and for fairly obvious reasons, critical theorists are interested in maintaining a democratic political system. What is very different, however, is how this overarching purpose translates into specific educational goals. Whereas schools have historically focused only on producing a kind of autopilot patriotism *(My country, right or wrong—but it's always right)*, critical theory suggests that schools instead try to educate active and thoughtful citizens, interested in having a voice in government and prepared to do so intelligently. Rather than defining patriotism as unquestioning loyalty, the critical theorist assumes a position articulated by John Dewey decades ago that suggests democracy is best protected not by rabid flag-wavers but by an active and skeptical public:

> Only through constant watchfulness and criticism of public officials by citizens can a state be maintained in integrity and usefulness. (1927, 69)

From this perspective, nurturing a patriotic citizen means encouraging a young person to actively question, rather than blindly obey, authority. In this vision for schools, educators act on the belief that the survival of democracy depends not on "bloated calls to force students to say the pledge of allegiance," but instead on schools' ability to nurture active and engaged citizens who will "be informed, make decisions, and . . . exercise control over the material and ideological forces" that shape their lives:

> [D]emocracy is not simply a lifeless tradition or disciplinary subject that is merely passed on from one generation to the next. . . . . [but something that] encourages all citizens to actively construct and share power over those institutions that govern their lives. (Giroux 1993, 12–13)

From this perspective, democracy is not a thing to revere, but a way of living.

In keeping with this definition of democracy as something to be lived rather than studied, a critical curriculum replaces the mindless parroting of patriotic rhetoric (which has taught countless children to pledge allegiance "to the republic of Richard Sands") with efforts to promote genuine civic understanding. Prominent educator Theodore Sizer both details such understanding and sees its potential for shaping a better United States when he argues that students must develop:

> a grasp of the basis for consensual democratic government, a respect for its processes, and acceptance of the restraints and obligations incumbent on a citizen. . . . if all American citizens had mastered at the least the complex principles [in the Bill of Rights], this would be a more just society. (1985, 86)

That the society could, and should, be more just is an integral tenet of critical theory, for reasons that will become evident in the following paragraphs.

To help students grow into knowledgeable and engaged citizens, the focus in a critical classroom is not on memorization but on questioning, on examining existing conditions and proposals with a skeptical eye—on the "watchfulness and criticism" that Dewey advocated. Always, the critical educator encourages such questions as *Who made this decision, who devised this plan, based on what criteria? Who will gain what from it? Who will lose what?* From a critical perspective, such questioning is essential because the status quo always privileges one segment of society over another, and the goal of the critical theorist is to promote a more genuinely equitable society—a society that more closely resembles the promise of democratic rhetoric, equal opportunity to all. The critical educator strives to ensure that every group of young people, the disenfranchised as well as the privileged—poor as well as rich; black and red and yellow as well as white; gay as well as straight; female as well as male—enjoys equal opportunity to pursue a better future through education. To that end, critical questioning purposefully challenges the status quo by examining it through the lens of the less privileged.

In schools, such questioning leads to challenges to long-revered curricular assumptions and routines:

> Whose history and literature is taught and whose ignored? Which groups are included and which left out of the reading list or text? From whose point of view is the past and present examined? Which themes are emphasized and which not? Is the curriculum balanced and multicultural, giving equal attention to men, women, minorities, and nonelite groups, or is it traditionally male-oriented and Eurocentric? Do students read about Columbus from the point of view of the Arawak people he conquered or only from the point of view of the Europeans he led into conquest? Do science classes investigate the biochemistry of the students' lives, like the nutritional value of the school lunch or the potential toxins in the local air, water, and land, or do they only talk abstractly about photosynthesis? (Shor 1992, 14)

The curricular implications here are clear and in sharp contrast to tradition.

The traditional educator, wanting students to support the status quo, will continue to quote T.S. Eliot and to insist that students can spell photosynthesis, as teachers have done for decades. In contrast, the critical educator, wanting students to broaden their experience and thinking, will introduce the voices of Sojourner Truth or Lame Deer, since a commitment to non-mainstream groups makes multiculturalism essential. Additionally, in a critical classroom, research becomes not something done by distant authorities in white lab coats, but by students themselves. As Freire suggests, for example, students might research local living conditions:

> Why not, for example, take advantage of the students' experience of life in those parts of the city neglected by the authorities to discuss the problems of pollution in the rivers and the question of poverty and the risks to health from the rubbish heaps in such areas? Why are there no rubbish heaps in the heart of the rich areas of the city? (1998, 36)

Incorporating such changes is a difficult process, however, because it threatens many, teachers and students alike, who are privileged by the status quo.

Questions like those above, for example, are considered "'in bad taste,'" as Freire himself notes (1998, 36); they call attention to conditions that citizens living in clean and safe neighborhoods would rather not think about. And, including multicultural voices in the curriculum suggests that other cultures may well have valuable ideas to offer. Honoring other cultures, however, challenges the presumed superiority of Anglo Saxon culture and implies that it's time for the mainstream to stop dismissing members of other cultures as uncivilized or savage. Some discomfort for those who currently enjoy a variety of privileges is inevitable, and so resistance is to be expected. Such resistance will be exacerbated as psychological discomfort is compounded by the prospect of economic change.

To suggest that business decisions should be based less on profitability and more on potential health and environmental concerns, for example, challenges the dominant assumption that profitability always matters most. The assumptions that critical educators challenge, like "We have the world's greatest culture" or "We *must* maximize profit" have been used by the powerful to their own advantage, often at significant material cost to the less powerful. For example, the unquestioned primacy of the bottom line allowed politicians in the 1980s to suggest that ketchup might count as a vegetable in school lunches, and even now, it allows American industries to continue puffing toxic gases into the air of industrial areas far removed from the sheltered enclaves of the wealthy and their children. The cigarette industry has profited from its blatant disregard of human health for decades, and the meat packing industry has similarly found it acceptable to maximize profit through unsafe practices that routinely not only injure but maim and kill employees (Killing

Zone 2002). The critical educators' agenda directly challenges the conditions produced by exclusive focus on profitability and in doing so, it threatens to decrease not only the sense of cultural superiority that the privileged enjoy, but also the excessive profits that allow for their material well-being.

The rhetorical results of such challenges to existing privilege are not surprising. (The same is true of practical results, but they will be detailed in later chapters.) Despite their commitment to sustaining democracy, critical theorists are often charged with "politicizing" education and promoting unpatriotic practices. Critical theorists themselves, of course, consider such charges nonsense, and they generally answer with the words of Paulo Freire: "education *is* politics!" (Shor & Freire 1987, 46, emphasis added). That is, there is no way to keep politics out of schools. There is also no way to disentangle political goals from economic ones. When schools support the status quo, as they have for almost two centuries, they are in fact supporting the political and economic goals of supporting current distribution of wealth, prestige and power; when they challenge the status quo, they are in fact pursuing a more equitable distribution of wealth, prestige and power—"a different distribution of material force and well-being than that which satisfies those now in control" (Dewey 1927, 119). Far from being unpatriotic, critical educators intend to make the democracy healthier by uncovering societal inequities and biases, promoting social responsibility, and effecting a more just and equitable society. Critical educators insist on including in classrooms the very criticism of the status quo that traditionalists work so hard to exclude.

Inevitably, such criticisms threaten both assumptions and practices essential to maintaining existing privilege. Not only do they call into question the current emphasis on maximum profitability at any cost, as indicated above, but they also challenge the deeply ingrained assumption that schools should be devoted to job training—especially to training hordes of docile workers to the specifications of business and industry.

As Joel Spring notes, "It is not necessarily true that what is good for American business is good for American schools and students" (1996, 24). Among the several reasons Spring offers to support this assertion, the most important is that when schools offer a curriculum specifically designed to meet the needs of employers, the effect is to help business ensure that they'll keep wages as low as possible—good for business, perhaps, but not for the students who will be tomorrow's workers. Wages often depend on the supply of labor; obviously, the more workers trained in a particular skill available to employers, the lower wages employers need to pay. From the standpoint of business, the ideal situation for hiring is a large pool of applicants that will allow business to pay the lowest wages and select the best worker. For example, in the 1950s business put pressure on the schools to educate more scientists and engineers and by the late 1960s there was a surplus of scientists and engineers, causing low wages and unemployment.

Rather than assuming that businesses have the right to dictate to schools the kinds of workers that are needed, critical educators ask questions about what kinds of jobs businesses are trying to fill and whether the worker or the employer is most likely to benefit substantively from such job preparation at public expense. The reality is that most public schools, especially in poor and working class neighborhoods, serve business interests rather than the interests of their students, increasing profits for employers while doing little to help workers significantly better their lives. (Contemporary examples of this assertion are detailed in Chapters Four and Five.)

Helping businesses keep wages low not only disadvantages students economically, but it often harms them psychologically, even spiritually, as well. It's all very well and good to say that hard work and a high school diploma lead to success, but when a particular region and a high school diploma offer graduates only jobs paying minimum wage—a wage that does not even allow a single parent to pay for child care during work hours—young people stop believing traditional rhetoric, and they stop trusting teachers and other authority figures who promote it. This disillusionment partly explains why so many disadvantaged students leave schools without graduating, virtually ensuring they will never legally improve their lives and simultaneously increasing their alienation from mainstream society.

> Teenagers are a throwaway generation, and they resent it. It is not for nothing that no age group has a higher crime rate. . . . In spite of the rhetoric to the contrary, they are largely tracked by social class and gender. Too few adults believe that poor kids or minority kids can make it. Don't educate their minds, the conventional wisdom goes, because they aren't interested, and anyway, we do them a big service by preparing them for (semiskilled) jobs. (Sizer 1985, 220)

As Barbara Ehrenreich (2001) so richly demonstrates in *Nickel and Dimed*—an account of her efforts to exist while working at a variety of minimum wage jobs—graduating from high school, qualifying for and obtaining the kinds of jobs abundantly available to the poor may not ensure them even minimal housing. Treating students so shabbily, offering them such a bleak and limited future, educators should not be surprised when disadvantaged young people start considering school and schooling irrelevant. For such students, the dreams of democracy become the dreams of the privileged Other, a fantasy—a lie—that the poor cannot afford to sustain.

Such disillusionment, the critical theorist would argue, poses the most significant threat to democracy. When the economically and educationally disenfranchised stop believing that our much vaunted democracy offers them real hope, then the entire society is at risk. If the dream of democracy is a fraud, why continue to support the existing government? If educational and economic opportunity is a myth, why not turn to welfare and welfare fraud, to drug use, to drug sales, to rioting, to looting—to countless activities that undermine the fabric of society? If, in fact, the American dream is a lie, if the existing system does not offer equal opportunity to those who not already in power, we should not be surprised when the disadvantaged use any means at their disposal to protest mainstream complicity in their disenfranchisement. After all: what do they have to lose?

Again, from a critical perspective the only hope for the future of the democracy is to encourage marginalized groups to develop the power and political will necessary to effect change in the existing systems that serve to keep them in their current places. This goal makes imperative an entirely new social agenda promoting a much wider range of values and viewpoints.

For example, rather than functioning as norms, docility and passivity become the enemies in a critical classroom, characteristics to be replaced with students' critical questioning and quest for self-determination. Rather than believing economic success comes only from hard work, and failure only from laziness, students must learn to ask what *besides* laziness might explain so many families living in poverty and the widening chasm between our wealthiest and poorest citizens. Rather than learning to *go along to get along* in a world not of their making, students must learn to decide for themselves what kind of future might best serve them, their families, and a country that promises equal opportunity to every constituent group.

The critical focus on questioning and self-determination inevitably produces a new social agenda for schools, because critical questioning applies to values as well as to everything else. Inevitably, such questioning challenges traditional values as solitary and unimpeachable criteria for decision-making. For example, as noted above, a willingness to work hard is considered an essential part of American character. However, in contemporary society the definition of a good person/worker as someone willing to work really, *really* hard has allowed many businesses to impose a "normal" work week of 60–80 hours on workers—to the enormous benefit not of the workers themselves, but of stockholders and other elite. "Mandatory overtime" has become routine in many industries, where workers have not had the option of a 40-hour work week in years. Two workers who each work 60 hours per week provide the company with an additional 40 hours of labor, allowing the company to hire one less person and to save the associated cost for benefits, always a major expense. Workers are forced into an unreasonable work schedule because it helps management save a great deal of money; any cost to the workers is considered unimportant next to the financial benefit to the company.

Currently, the idea that working hard means relinquishing an excessive amount of one's time is so widespread that even organizations beyond business have begun to capitalize on it. College football coaches have been skirting NCAA regulations intended to protect players' health and welfare by scheduling "voluntary" practices beyond the hours allowed. Officially, players don't have to attend, but they know that if they don't attend, they are likely to be punished by not playing. Like factory workers, players have accepted the need to give more of themselves than is reasonable. Only the related deaths of two Florida players within five months have brought such "voluntary" practices under public scrutiny (Berkow 2001).

While the current cultural definition of "hard work" has become a very profitable tool for authorities, abuses like those above prompt the critical theorist to question various facets of the contemporary veneration of "hard work": What is the cost of current practices to workers in terms of their health, personal interests, relationships, and family lives? By what right does any authority presume the right to such a vast proportion of anyone else's life? Do work contracts make clear how much of a worker's life will be required? Or, do unwritten and unspoken rules allow authorities to consume the lives of others and undermine their well-being even as they trumpet their commitment to the welfare of those under their control?

Such questions propose not that we discard such traditional values as hard work, but that we consciously examine how they are being defined and implemented. The critical theorist urges that we consider balancing them against other values that are equally legitimate: the need to work hard with the need to maintain a healthy and happy personal life; the need to compete with the need to cooperate; the need for business to make a profit with the need for business to behave ethically; the need to obey laws in a civilized society with the need to challenge and change unfair and unjust laws; the need to cultivate a common American identity with the need to ensure that that identity comfortably fits all of our many citizens. These kinds of balance, often fostered by examining the values paramount in other cultures (like the Native American emphasis on conservation) will open new possibilities much better calibrated to serve the needs of all American constituencies, not just a powerful few.

In this insistence that education serve the interests of the many rather than the few, the critical theorist offers a vision and an agenda far more democratic and patriotic than its privileged critics will ever admit.

The Why and How of Praxis

Unlike the contemporary politician, the critical theorist does not believe that a productive one-size-fits-all curriculum and assessment system is possible. Of course all students need to learn to read and write and calculate, but those processes are far less defined than many assume. What are students to read? (the *Scarlet Letter* and *Tale of Two Cities*? Chief Joseph's last speech? *The Joy Luck Club*? editorials in the local newspaper?) What are they to write? (answers to factual questions about the Globe Theatre? answers to textbook questions in the words of the text? original poetry? their own letters to the editor?) What are they to calculate? (how soon two speeding trains will pass in the night? household budgets for a single parent earning minimum wage? the number of children who go to bed hungry based on national poverty percentages?)

Critical educators believe that all such curricular decisions must be based on classroom context. Many choices, of course, are between the content of a traditional curriculum and the content of a critical curriculum. But even within a critical classroom, there are no standard answers. For example, while it is equally important for both privileged and non-privileged students to understand current inequities, their different life experiences require different pedagogical approaches. Students in Oregon might gain a better understanding of their own lives by reading from the speeches of Chief Joseph, while students in California might reach the same goal more efficiently by reading works by Amy Tan or Richard Rodriguez. Classroom discussions informed by such works would also vary. While privileged students might ask themselves how their mainstream status protected them from challenges minority writers faced, marginalized groups might focus instead on the price of trying to remake themselves in the mainstream WASP image.

For this reason, and to the chagrin of many traditionally educated teachers, critical theorists and educators have no standard curriculum and pedagogy to offer. Instead of saying, as traditionalists so often do, "Here's the way to do *xyz* in the classroom," critical educators speak instead of *praxis:* action based upon reflection, the kind of reflection this text supports. No one can tell a critical educator what issue will be most compelling and which strategies most productive in his or her individual classroom. Instead, each teacher must develop individual praxis by first analyzing his or her own context and then designing appropriate, context-specific curricula and strategies.

Recently, good books that describe individual critical classrooms and pedagogies have become available (Shor & Pari 1999, for example). However, it is important for readers to understand that such books do not provide formulas for critical pedagogy. Instead, they tell the stories of how individual teachers arrived at praxis for their own classrooms. The value of these narratives is not in offering class plans for duplication, but in illustrating the path to praxis. This path is always individual, and it always begins with a classroom practitioner identifying a compelling issue in his or her own classroom. For J. Alleyne Johnson, for example, passing by the scene of a shooting led to a new awareness of how death pervades her students' lives and how difficult their lives are. Haunted by the incident, Johnson eventually acted by offering her students a voice in curriculum and they chose to develop a class newspaper. The final product contained several carefully crafted student pieces relevant to the relentless presence of death in their lives. Johnson ends the narrative not by suggesting that all other teachers rush out and begin assigning class newspapers, but instead by stressing the importance of praxis. Rather than trying to impose a single standard and curriculum on students, as the traditionalist educator insists, Johnson stresses the need to adapt classrooms to the specific students who people them, as critical educators urge:

> Whether we as teachers choose to address it or not, students' lives come with them to school, death and other aspects of students' realities come into our classrooms. Instead of wishing for other students, let us gear our work towards the students we have. (49)

Recipes simply are not possible in a critical classroom. Each teacher must undertake a conscious analysis of every element of an individual teaching situation and design action based on that analysis; that is to say, again, every teacher must develop a personal praxis.

The process, however, is fraught with both difficulty and danger, and so educators who choose a critical path must do so with eyes wide open, with the thorough understanding of practical consequences that this text seeks to nurture. Many teachers, for example, are privileged themselves, and they need first to develop an awareness of their own privilege, a difficult and threatening undertaking detailed in Chapter Two.

It's easy to say we all want the poor to have more—much harder to accept the reality of others having less as a result. It's easy to say we want to end discrimination—much harder to accept that the *Koran* and the *Dhammapada* merit places alongside the *Bible*. It's easy to say that students must learn to use their own voices—much harder to give up our own authority over curriculum to students.

And, the educator who implements critical pedagogy is likely to incur the resistance of privileged Others—colleagues, administrators, politicians and religious groups among them—at considerable professional risk. It's easy to say that the disapproval of others will be no big deal—much harder to maintain a new pedagogy when former friendly colleagues become lunchroom adversaries, or when administrators and parents turn hostile in a meeting challenging classroom activities.

Readers will find much in later chapters that is discouraging, because the forces shaping existing conditions are well-funded, powerful, and deeply entrenched. However, readers who see the advantages of critical alternatives but nevertheless fear that their reform efforts might be futile or too costly need to remember this: accepting traditional practice without resistance also has a very high cost. Since education *is* politics, no choice is neutral, and all choices have consequences—and so there simply is no neutral ground for an educator to stand on. Teachers who just go along, who never think about the assumptions underpinning their practice, in effect drift with local current, and by their drifting they travel a route charted by others. Teachers committed to a higher standard of professionalism must instead thoughtfully choose a direction, must mindfully and consciously enter one of two metaphorical rivers Shor sketches:

Two great rivers of reform are flowing in opposite directions across the immense landscapes of American education. One river flows from the top down and the other from the bottom up. The top-down river has been the voice of authority proposing conservative agendas that support inequality and traditional teaching; the bottom-up flow contains multicultural voices speaking for social justice and alternative methods. These two rivers represent different politics, different models for teaching and learning, and finally different visions of the people and society we should build through education. Will conservative agendas succeed in imposing more control, more rote learning, and more unequal funding on public education? Or will emerging groups and networks democratically remake school systems especially divided by race and class, from impoverished inner cities to affluent suburbs to depressed rural areas? (Shor & Pari 1999, vii)

While this may not be a choice that education students and today's educators bargained for when they decided to enter the profession, it is an inescapable choice nonetheless.

In its entirety, this text seeks to provide sufficient impetus and information for readers to choose thoughtfully and consciously.

Note

1. Students were subsequently invited to perform the play at Broadway's Roundabout Theater and did so to a near capacity crowd.

For Further Reading

Fine, M., & Weis, L. (2003). *Silenced voices and extraordinary conversations . . . Re-imagining schools*. New York: Teachers College Press.

Hinchey, P. (1998). *Finding freedom in the classroom: A practical introduction to critical theory.* New York: Peter Lang Publishing.

Kohn, A. (1999). Forward . . . into the past. *Rethinking Schools Online, 14*(1). Available at http://www.rethinkingschools.org.

Parker, W. (Ed.). (2002). *Education for democracy: Contexts, curricula, assessments.* Greenwich, CT: Information Age Publishing.

Spring, J. (2000). *The American School 1642—2000* (5th ed.). New York: McGraw-Hill.

CHAPTER 2

Understanding Our Own Thinking: Developing Critical Consciousness

The accomplishment of critical consciousness consists in the first place in the learner's capacity to situate herself in her own historicity, for example, to grasp the class, race, and sexual aspects of education and social formation.

PAULO FREIRE

To make a fully-informed choice between conservative and critical practice, educators must cultivate a wide variety of understandings, including an understanding of how their thinking is shaped by their own position in and experiences with American culture. We act based on what we believe, and what we believe depends in large part upon evidence drawn from our own life experiences.

For example, people who attended a school where it was normal for everyone to show up every day are likely to become adults, possibly teachers, who simply expect that students enrolled in school will show up there regularly. For them, going to school every day is a *normal* activity. However, people who attended schools where only a third of the students enrolled routinely showed up on any given day are likely to have very different expectations and a very different definition of *normal* school attendance. Teachers who develop classroom plans based solely on beliefs and expectations born of their own life experiences are likely to be ineffective in, and probably very frustrated by, a school where others with different experiences have different norms.

It is particularly important for teachers to ask how their particular backgrounds have shaped their thinking because as a group, teachers are strikingly homogeneous. Their similar backgrounds and experiences make it likely that their thinking on important issues, like the goals of education or standards for student behavior, will also be similar. However, vast numbers of school children come from ethnic and socio-economic backgrounds very different from their teachers', and so they are likely to bring very different assumptions, expectations, and norms to the classroom.

At least in part because most teachers have middle-class backgrounds, for example, teachers commonly believe that schooling ensures students will get decent jobs. After all, teachers are likely to know many people (including themselves) who completed high school and college and found satisfactory jobs. But unlike the middle class teachers, students who live in urban ghettos or poor rural communities are likely to know many people who earned a high school diploma but never found a decent job within a practical distance. The car, or the subway or bus or train, that provides the mobility the middle-class takes for granted is not available to many of the nation's poor, though many teachers are unaware of that reality. Their job opportunities are constrained by distance, and most often there are few desirable jobs within geographical reach. The fact is that students from poor communities often have their own very strong evidence that schooling is not likely to make a significant difference in their futures, a belief that strongly affects their behavior.

The reality of American society is that students who come from a home and family that is "other"—that is non-White and/or non-middle class and/or non-native English speaking—have very good reasons to have a significantly different perception of education. Even for those who do well academically, education is not necessarily the magical cure for inequity many suppose. In 1993, for example, the *Los Angeles Times* reported that:

> Whether they have dropped out of high school or invested years in a graduate degree, whether they have struggled to master English or not, California's minorities earn substantially less than Anglos—a disparity that challenges the long-held tenet that education is a key to equality. In fact, the gap between Anglo and minority earnings widens among some of the most educated Californians . . . Although all workers earn more if they stay in school, the return on investment is substantially larger for Anglos. The bachelor's degree that, on average, adds more than $17,000 to a typical Anglo's pay is worth less than $12,500 to the average African-American. And the professional credential that boosts a college-educated Anglo's salary by about $33,000 a year is worth less than half that to the average Latino—even if he or she is born in the United States. (Hubler & Silverstein 1)

One reason that it's important for teachers from the White mainstream to become aware of the impact of their own backgrounds, then, is that some key assumptions they've never questioned, like the value of education being a self-evident truth, may well be in direct opposition to their students' perceptions and assumptions. Often, such oppositional assumptions lead to classroom tension and conflict.

Additionally, the homogeneity of the teaching force is a critical issue because it imposes fairly rigid expectations on teachers, who may well not understand how these expectations influence their thinking and behavior. The existing teaching force embodies an unarticulated template that dictates what kind of people will become teachers, what kind of people will teach which grades and subjects, and what kind of people will be responsible for policies governing classroom activity. The overwhelming majority of the teaching force is comprised of teachers who conform to these traditional expectations and who are likely to feel very much at home in the profession. They are also likely, however, to be unaware of the extent to which they are enacting someone else's cultural agenda. Meanwhile, those few teachers who do not happen to match the template in such areas as gender, class, race and socio-economic status find themselves—hardly for the first time—part of a nearly invisible and often devalued minority. Neither majority nor minority teachers will be able to choose among options freely until they have examined how their membership in either of those groups may have affected their thinking, especially in terms of what is normal, or right or good, for teachers, students, and schools.

The critical theorist calls such understandings *critical consciousness,* which includes an awareness that our ideas come from a particular set of life experiences, an ability to trace our ideas to their sources in our experience, and an acknowledgement that others will have equally valid, if different, life experiences and ideas. Most importantly, developing critical consciousness involves accepting that ideas about what is normal, or right, or good, are the products of life experience rather than universal laws. It is normal to value education if your life experience offers evidence that education is a route to success; however, it is equally normal, however much teachers may want to discount or bemoan the fact, to scorn education if your life experience offers evidence that for others like you, education has proven a dead end.

Critical questioning of life experience and personal beliefs is a difficult and threatening process for anyone, but especially for those with a mainstream background, because the process frequently generates challenges to our most cherished cultural beliefs—especially the beliefs that America provides everyone with equal opportunity and that people ultimately reap no more and no less than they have earned. Those who fit the cultural template and who have succeeded are well-schooled in the idea that others had the same opportunities. For such successful people as teachers, accepting that success might depend on anything other than personal merit means that they must at least consider the possibility that their own success is due not only to their own merit but also to cultural bias in their favor.

Few educators are willing to undertake such a painful mental journey and to make such a painful admission. In fact, Quiocho and Rios (2000) suggest that teacher and administrator reluctance to analyze the influence of their personal histories helps maintain the mistaken idea that schools can be politically neutral:

The failure to employ political clarity about school structures is due, in part, to workers (principally teachers and administrators) who are captives of their own socioocultural experiences whether they realize it or not. This failure exists, in part, because many school-based professionals are unwilling to critique an ideology and structure that may jeopardize their own position of privilege.

For many teachers, the path to critical consciousness will result in an unhappy new awareness of unacknowledged and unearned privilege. It may also reveal equally unfair biases and roadblocks. But no matter the specific results, the process of examining formerly unconscious assumptions is never easy or pleasant, because it always requires a move out of our comfort zone and into unfamiliar territory. Unpleasant as this prospect might be, teachers with a sincere commitment to making informed professional choices have no choice but to ask themselves hard questions about their own experiences and assumptions. To do otherwise is to choose professional blindness and to drift on a current of complacency at a time when children desperately need their teachers to be charting the future of education thoughtfully and ethically.

The remainder of this chapter provides information that may help readers begin to explore the difficult path toward critical consciousness, which is not a destination but a lifelong process, and which is a necessary precursor to consciously defining a professional identity. Highlighted below are personal characteristics that inevitably, and often unconsciously, influence life experience and thinking both before and after a person enters the teaching profession: race, gender, language, class and sexual orientation. Of course, this is a highly selective and fully inadequate list of influences, and it is far beyond the scope of this text to deal adequately with these areas, whose complexities are being probed in a steadily growing literature. I trust that readers already familiar with these issues will recognize the following simplifications as intended for a reader who has not yet begun interrogating his or her own sociocultural experience.

Issues of Race

A 2002 U.S. Census Bureau report, based on 1993–94 statistics, indicates that as a group, public school teachers are overwhelmingly White. According to this report, White teachers in public schools outnumber teachers of color by a ratio of nearly 8: 1. More specifically, White teachers outnumber Black teachers about 12:1 and Hispanics by about 20:1. Not surprisingly, teacher education students are also overwhelmingly White. Few members of even the largest minority, African Americans, appear in teacher education classrooms, especially at predominantly White institutions:

In 1989, African Americans made up 6.8% of undergraduate students enrolled in teacher education programs, compared with 86.5% for White students (Hood & Parker 1994). In 1991, African Americans made up 6.6% of undergraduate students enrolled in teacher education programs, compared with 86.4% for White students (AACTE, 1994). The percentage of African American undergraduate students enrolled in teacher education programs jumped to 9% in 1995, with approximately one third (33.7%) of these students enrolled in teacher education programs at historically Black colleges and universities (HBCUs) (AACTE, 1999). Of all bachelor's degree recipients in the 1993–1994 academic year, 86% were White and 6% were African American (AACTE, 1999). Thus, HBCUs are the primary training ground for African American teachers; when compared with White students, African American students are not equitably represented in college overall or in teacher education programs specifically. (Wilder 2000)

In terms of what is normal and not normal in the profession and in teacher education classrooms, then, normal—like the national template—is White.

As Katz describes the situation:

When news media proclaim that public schools in the United States are becoming more ethnically diverse, they tend to ignore the fact that only one segment of the school population is changing: the students and their families, who come from an increasingly varied array of ethnic, cultural, and linguistic backgrounds. Though children of color and their families make up the largest segment of this population in terms of numbers of stakeholders at a given site, it is another group of stakeholders—those who teach in its classrooms or lead the weekly assemblies—who tend to make the critical decisions about what happens in schools such as what gets taught and how, whose voices get heard, and how classrooms are constituted. The demographics of these members of the school community have, for the most part, remained the same; today's teachers are mostly White. (1999, 496)

Despite the fact that people of color now constitute half or more of the United States population, the teaching profession mirrors the national White template. This skewed racial representation means that most public school teachers come from significantly different cultures than their students and that as a group, they enjoy unacknowledged privileges denied to many of their students.

Being oblivious to the many privileges of their race keeps teachers ignorant of some of the most basic realities of their students' lives. Perhaps the most startling among these is the ability to go through life blissfully unaware of their skin color as anything particularly important. Of course people with white skin know they have it, but that is not the same thing as acknowledging Whiteness as an America standard, or realizing the privileges Whiteness brings, or being aware of the daily frustrations and challenges that people of color face. Because of the strength of the cultural template and the depth to which it is embedded in countless elements of daily life, it is a significant challenge for any White person even to become aware of the effects of his or her own Whiteness.

I am acutely aware of how strange these statements will sound to many readers, likely to be White themselves given the demographics detailed above, because I myself was well into my middle years before I developed any awareness of my own Whiteness. I recognized my younger self fairly recently when a Black discussion leader asked a group of educators when they'd become conscious of what their skin color meant. Generally, my White colleagues responded with confusion, unable to understand the question. As I've detailed in another piece of writing, in contrast to my White colleagues, I had a ready answer:

> . . . "I learned I was White, to my amazement, only some 10 years ago, during the last days of my doctoral program, when I was approaching my 40th birthday." Now, there is nothing tricky about either my appearance or my ethnicity—I am a blue-eyed, light skinned blonde, 100% Caucasian . . . [And so, many will answer my statement with their own incredulity:] "That's ridiculous. You couldn't possibly have lived decades without knowing you were White . . ."
>
> The background of my remark demonstrates, I think, the world of difference between having some information about oneself ("I am a Caucasian") and developing a sense of [what critical theorists call] historicity ("Having light skin and being classified as Caucasian has resulted in my noticing this and ignoring that in my daily life; in believing this and that about what constitutes *normal;* and in naming this thing good and that thing *not good").*
>
> When exactly did I learn I was White? On holiday break from a new full-time job in New York City, when I visited my local mall back home in northeastern Pennsylvania and observed to myself "Boy, there sure are a lot of White people here!"
>
> The thought literally stopped me dead in my tracks.
>
> I was shopping in a place I'd visited countless times: *Why had that particular thought never once occurred to me before?* How could I have been swimming in a sea of White and never *seen* it? Why did I suddenly notice an *absence* of color that I'd been oblivious to my entire life?
>
> (Hinchey 2001)

The answer is that a life spent in White communities with other White people, and in a culture where a pervasive media presents White images as the norm, makes having White skin—for those who have it—just a normal part of life, nothing exceptional, nothing worth paying any attention to.

That the ability to forget about skin color is a White privilege becomes evident only when we start to analyze places where the routine experiences of Whites contrast with the routine experiences of people of color. In a well-known article, Peggy McIntosh (1990) catalogues some typical and widely unacknowledged privileges that come with White skin. Listing her own privileges, she includes:

- I can go shopping alone most of the time, pretty well assured that I will not be followed or harassed.
- When I am told about our national heritage or about "civilization," I am shown that people of my color made it what it is.
- I can be sure that my children will be given curricular materials that testify to the existence of their race.
- I can arrange to protect my children most of the time from people who might not like them.
- I am never asked to speak for all the people in my racial group.
- I can take a job with an affirmative action employer without having coworkers on the job suspect that I got it because of race.
- I can be sure that if I need legal or medical help my race will not work against me.
- I can remain oblivious of the language and customs of persons of color, who constitute the world's majority, without feeling in my culture any penalty for such oblivion.

Many Whites don't consider such factors *privileges* because they've always had the luxury of taking them for granted. People of color, however, are confronted daily with a far different reality. They are often followed and harassed in stores; they cannot protect their children from similar experiences or from verbal abuse; others often assume that they are not well-qualified for a job they hold; they rarely see their race represented in history books or in the highest levels of authority. And, they can largely count on the fact that Whites will know little about their widely different cultures, confusing Jamaicans with Tanzanians and Mexicans with Puerto Ricans.

Adding insult to injury, individual people of color from a single group are often expected to tutor Whites about the kaleidoscope of cultures represented by all people of color, everywhere. Dismayed by a departmental discussion of race, one educator of color wrote to her supervisor detailing the enormity of simply having a skin color other than White:

> It is the thing you can never get away from, the label that others give you that they won't ever release and they won't let you forget. Can you imagine the constant confrontation of the issue of race permeating every day of your life for one reason or another? (Over representation or under representation of people who look like you do in whatever arena, the blatant inequities in quality of life for the masses—educational opportunities, housing, ability to pass down wealth or privilege, the stinging humiliations that come from the mouths or pens of others who may or may not be well-intentioned, IQ scores being thrown in your face, etc.) It is reality for us. It is not a discussion, not a theory. It is flesh and blood. . . . (Cochran-Smith 2000)

Unlike Whites, persons of color never have the luxury of forgetting about their skin color or considering it an unimportant factor in daily life.

Only when something they've always considered normal comes into open conflict with what they experience as real do Whites generally become conscious of their race. This is the case when a White teacher finds him or herself in a school at odds with the neighborhoods and classrooms they formerly hadn't bothered to imagine:

> White teachers may experience some form of culture shock (Dworkin, 1987) when they find themselves in unfamiliar mismatched contexts where they are the minority. (Mueller, Finley, Iverson, & Price 1999)

Part of this culture shock comes from Whites being deprived for the first time of many of the privileges their race has allowed them to take for granted for decades:

> What we can say is that White teachers in contexts where others are of the same race receive greater coworker support, experience less role conflict, have greater autonomy in decision making, and have adequate resources. (Mueller, Finley, Iverson, & Price 1999)

Not surprisingly, these researchers further report that "These better work conditions then increase their job satisfaction and commitment to their school." Generally, White teachers expect that their professional colleagues will look and sound like them, will share similar values, will define the purpose of education and will explain poor student performance in much the same ways. Only being deprived of unrecognized privileges that come with being part of a majority population nudges many Whites to notice the very different experience of being a racial minority. And, not surprisingly, they are not happy when they find themselves in the minority.

In short, "Race matters," as prominent Black scholar Cornel West has written (1993), and it matters a great deal in classrooms, not only to Whites, as suggested above, but also to persons of color. Not surprisingly, lifelong experience in an American culture that presents Whiteness as the cultural norm spares the few teachers of color who do make their way into White classrooms the same kind of culture shock that Whites experience when they are the minority:

> Individuals who are accustomed to being in the minority in society (Blacks in White-dominant situations) are not negatively affected by being in mismatched contexts. Black teachers seem to have adapted to the variety of racial contexts they find themselves in. (Mueller, Finley, Iverson, & Price 1999)

The fact that individual people of color may be accustomed to minority status in White groups does not, however, mean that they face no particular challenges when they choose teaching as a profession.

In fact, the invisibility of people of color and suspicion of them that McIntosh notes as characteristic of the culture at large are also reflected in student experience, as Karla Lewis notes:

> At times I felt as if I did not belong in college. Initially, I felt like I belonged, but it did not take long to realize that I did not. White people I barely knew asked me what I got on my scholastic aptitude test and about my high school grade point average. I was really being asked, "Do you really belong here, or are you here to fill some two for affirmative action edict?" On my campus, with a total student population of 10,000, the African American student population was recorded at 4%. This meager enrollment percentage included graduate and undergraduate students. I thought that no one knew how isolated I felt and how difficult my situation was—there was only one other Black female in my dorm! (Willis & Lewis 1999)

At this moment in time, a person of color who pursues teaching as a career is sure to find himself or herself in an isolated national, and probably institutional, minority. And, that fact generates not only the challenges that all people of color face, like those just detailed, but it also translates into still other hurdles for minorities who want to become teachers.

In fact, the White norms permeating education at every level generate significant barriers that maintain the current racial imbalance in the teaching force. It is these culturally constructed barriers, and not lack of interest, that largely account for the scarcity of non-mainstream teachers. In fact, Quiocho and Rios (2000) report that, despite such hindrances as low regard for the teaching profession, high cost of college tuition, lack of role models, and high school tracking, many people of color are in fact attracted to teaching as a "way to make a substantial difference in their communities":

> This latter reason for seeking teaching as a profession may rest on minority group people's perceptions that schools cheat minority students and serve the aspirations of Euro-Americans (Su, 1997); indeed, their own experiences with prejudice in schooling may lead them to this conclusion (Klassen & Carr, 1997). Many minority group teachers believe that they can work to counteract this situation by establishing a culturally relevant and multiculturally inclusive curriculum (Su, 1997) and by helping to transform society (challenge the status quo) to counteract perceived unequal opportunities in schooling (Hood & Parker, 1994; Su, 1997).

Many of these potential teachers never have a chance to attempt to realize their intentions, however, because the White nature of schools and teacher preparation both function to keep even minorities with a keen interest in teaching out of the profession and out of classrooms.

First, teacher education students of color learn rapidly that their vision of educational goals is very different from their White professors' and student colleagues':

Starting out, then, many ethnic minority teachers might be at odds with the perspectives of most other professionals at the school site around issues of anti-racism as a goal of schooling. In a survey of 70 secondary teachers regarding anti-racist education, Klassen and Carr (1997) found that such education was supported differently by different teachers. Whereas minority teachers had direct experience with racism in their lives and supported anti-racist education, Euro-American teachers were (in the main) unaware of prejudices and thus did not support anti-racist education. (Quiocho & Rios 2000)

Morever, not surprisingly, minority education students also find themselves dismayed by a curriculum that, like their elementary and secondary school curricula, embodies the thoroughly White cultural template. Summarizing research on curricula in teacher education program, Quichos and Rios (2000) report that

> Lack of attention to (critical) diversity issues has resulted in many minority group students' feeling ill prepared to deal with diversity in school contexts. Hood and Parker's (1994) informants communicated the degree to which they felt unprepared to deal with issues of cultural diversity in the classroom based on their own lack of experience with a culturally relevant curriculum in their teacher education program. For these students, the only chance to deal with issues of diversity came in multicultural education courses and periodically in foundation classes. Overall, they felt that they faced a Euro-American middle-class orientation in their preparation for the teaching profession, they often believed that superficial attention was focused on diversity issues, and they perceived that Euro-American students' biases about ethnic minority people went unchallenged. Disturbingly, these minority group students reported that they also detected racist assumptions held by their professors (Hood & Parker, 1994).

Coming to teacher education with their own ideas about education as a lever to promote equity, minority candidates quickly learn that their goals are at odds with the intentions and content of most teacher education programs and professors.

It is for this reason that many of the minority students who choose to pursue teaching as a career do so at HBCUs, or historically Black colleges and universities, where the curriculum better matches their own ideas about schools and teaching. But ironically, even a more relevant curriculum doesn't help ensure the success of minority teaching candidates because being White, or having experiences that match the White experience as closely as possible, appears to be the greatest criteria for successful entry to the profession: White students routinely pass standardized teaching tests, while students of color routinely fail them. Consider these statistics for the Praxis exams, the commercial, standardized tests that many states require for certification:

> When Latham, Gitomer & Ziomek (1999) studied the passing rates of whites and minority candidates in the Praxis I and II from 1995–1997, they found that 82% of all

white candidates passed the Praxis I, as opposed to 46% of the African American candidates. For the Praxis II, 91 % of the white candidates passed as opposed to 69% of African American candidates. (Albers 2002)

Newspapers and legislators, of course, insist that the exams are fair and reasonable, and if students fail them, then the fault is with a poor educational program and an unprepared candidate. In fact, it has become increasingly common for such public voices to start calling for the dismantling of teacher education programs whose students—notably students of color—do not do well on the exams.

Albers (2002) and others make the case, however, that it is the test and not the student that is inadequate, that the fault lies not in the students but in the cultural bias of the texts toward Euro-Americans:

These pencil-and-paper tests, Hilliard (1984) argues, are inherently discriminatory and biased, and do not focus on what teaching entails: skills, attitudes, and understandings . . . . National tests, as Kemple and others (1995) contend, continue to focus on European-American cultural knowledge, and [W]hite teacher candidates tend to perform better on them. Schaeffer (1996) agrees, "the [teacher] tests are skewed in ways that result in huge numbers of people of color failing as compared to whites" and "result [s] in tens of thousands of Blacks and Latinos being excluded from the teaching force."

Students of Albers who failed the subject exam for secondary English teachers reported just such bias, and their experience makes clear how the pervasiveness of the White template miscasts the ability of students of color.

Each of the students Albers reports on had completed at least two graduate English courses, five graduate education courses, and a variety of field experiences. Each had successfully worked in classrooms with teachers who reported them as outstanding candidates. How could they fail a standardized exam? By not having a White cultural experience:

All of the African American teacher candidates noted what they believed to be a disproportionate number of questions about literature by [W]hite authors and literature by nonwhite authors in the content knowledge test. Alivia, Sentenio, Charles, and Kenisha remembered that the test had anywhere from six to nine questions (out of approximately 66) that dealt specifically with African American or nonwhite literature. After taking the Praxis II, Charles describes a conversation he had with another test-taker:

She was white, and I could tell she came from a conservative type of background. And we talked a little bit and she was very nice, but she was really upset over these questions [about African American authors]. She asked, "Okay, who wrote *Go Tell It on the Mountain?* Was it Richard Wright?" And I said, "Nooooo! James Baldwin." And she's like, "Oh!" So I could show off about this. Alicia, too, recalls one white teacher candidate's shock that the Praxis II would have a question about Lorraine Hansberry's *Raisin in the Sun:* "The teacher was so surprised that there would be a question about this text on this type of exam."

After taking the test, Charles wondered if [W]hite teacher candidates felt the same discomfort about answering questions on African American authors as he did with white authors. His ability to "show off" his knowledge of such questions made him wonder: This [conversation] made me start thinking about the other students [who] were complaining about there being too many African American questions on there. I honestly realized that I had a small advantage in the African American part just by being African American. I don't know if that's possible but it seems true. I mean, these [African American author] questions were driving the other [White] students crazy. And every African American that I talked to was so happy and so elated that these questions were on there. I mean like they were shoe-ins for us . . . . And I wondered if it would be the other way around. If the shoe was on the other foot, would I be happy to get these other questions? Would it be easier? It just made me think.

Cultural heroes and cultural treasures differ—but Whites have most of the power in the United States, and so White heroes and White cultural treasures have become the standard for curricula and for testing and students of color who know less about White culture than about their own culture pay dearly on exams, where their cultural knowledge is discounted. The point Charles makes above is one White readers should consider: If "the shoe [were] on the other foot," how many White students would be able to identify August Wilson, Ernest J. Gaines, W. E. B. DuBois, Zora Neale Hurston, Sojourner Truth, or John Lee Hooker? Or Lame Deer, N. Scott Momaday, Leslie Marmon Silko or R. Carlos Nakai?

There is a nasty cycle occurring here: Most public schools are based on a White template that neither applies to nor interests many minority students, who therefore don't take the schools seriously and become unsuccessful students. To alleviate this problem, some successful minority students pursue teaching, hoping they will be able to help create schools more attuned to the students who people them. Part of what they hope to take into schools is knowledge that can help minority students develop some cultural pride and some reassurance that schooling is relevant to them. However, they find that teacher education curricula and standardized testing are so saturated with White norms that rather than being empowered by pursuing teaching as a career, they are often debilitated by the experience.

Each of the African-American teacher education students Albers introduces was highly successful on any number of criteria outside the standardized exams, and yet each was seriously damaged by the experience of failure. Disheartened herself by the failure of these outstanding students, Albers reflects:

They walked into the Praxis II exam full of confidence about their academic preparation; however, after receiving their test scores, this confident feeling dissolved into disbelief, devastation, and embarrassment. . . . Just a year ago, these teacher candidates entered our program, full of enthusiasm, vigor, and life. They were passionate about the profession that they had chosen to pursue and eager to work with inner-city students in preparing them for life challenges. They continuously demonstrated their ability to teach through positive field-based experiences, their ability to take on the day-to-day challenges of teaching, and their commitment to the importance of culturally responsive teaching, especially with reluctant and/or resistant learners who themselves feel invisible in school. However, in just four short hours, a teacher test called the Praxis II nearly destroyed the qualities in them that we most value in teachers: confidence, knowledge of content, and a desire to work with students in a culturally responsive way. (2002)

As in the culture at large, students pay a high price for failing to match the pervasive White template—although they may well blame themselves rather than a biased culture for their failure. And, these circumstances in turn present teacher educators interested in equity a dilemma that will not be easy to resolve:

Do HBCUs or school/college of education that value multiculturalism, and the need for social justice acquiesce and align their curricula so that their teacher candidates can pass the Praxis II, a test that primarily values the language and literature of white authors? Or do they, as Ladson-Billings (1994) suggests, hold fast to their principles and continue to teach in a culturally responsive way, integrating fully the values and traditions presented in the literature and language of many authors of color? (Albers 2002)

Teacher educators' answers to these questions will shape the experiences of students of all colors, in colleges as well as K-12 institutions. There is no way to keep racial influences and issues out of classrooms at any level.

One step toward critical consciousness, then, is for the reader to begin paying attention to race in their own experience and in schools—on both sides of the classroom desk. What color are the people with most power, the people making the choices, setting the curriculum? Who is enjoying which advantages, who is enduring which challenges, simply because of their race? And most importantly: what is the color of the skin on the hands turning the pages of this book? And what difference has that made in what in his or her life experience and thinking?

Issues of Gender and Sexual Orientation

Another element key in shaping teachers' perspectives is gender. In addition to being a White profession, teaching is a gendered profession, with a distinct majority of teachers being women. According to the 2002 Census Bureau report, in 1993–94, females in the profession outnumbered men nearly 3:1 (Public Elementary). The situation is most apparent in elementary schools, where 84% of all teachers are female; in contrast, 51% of all high school teachers are male. Not coincidentally, elementary school subjects are widely considered the easiest to learn and to teach, and teaching in elementary school is generally thought to offer little intellectual challenge. Also not coincidentally, secondary school curricula are considered much more challenging to learn and difficult to teach.

An interesting dynamic is reflected here: historical, stereotypical thinking about women and women's roles have reified many ideas about a woman's "natural" character, widely assumed to include an innate tendency to nurture the young. Such stereotypical thinking helps explain why teaching, which places an adult in charge of children, is generally considered "women's work," most especially at the elementary level. Historically, although women's work (teaching, nursing, routine office work) has been devalued and underpaid, women have gladly accepted it as a way to pursue both financial and intellectual autonomy (Biklen 1995; Tamboukou 2000). And also historically, cultural stereotypes have followed women into classrooms and shaped their experiences there. Often, not only are female teachers bound in tightly restricted roles, as they are in other professions, but their own culturally induced and unexamined assumptions help perpetuate their subordinate roles inside and outside of schools.

Despite years of research and reports documenting gender role stereotyping and limitations placed upon women (Grumet 1988; Sadker & Sadker 1994; Biklen 1995), and like women in general, teacher education students—primarily White and primarily female—generally refuse to believe that gender plays any role in their experience and in classrooms. One education professor trying to help students begin to explore the path to critical consciousness reports:

> The most controversial segments of foundation courses are those that address issues of gender. . . . Both males and females angrily resent any suggestion that their perception of the world is incomplete or that their own individualistic experience is not sufficient to nullify a social pattern. When students are faced with values and beliefs that call into question their ideological frameworks, they deny that women constitute an oppressed group, no matter the structural barriers they might experience to their own success. (Titus 2000)

My own experience offers a supporting anecdote: I once had a female student with five siblings insist that there had been no gender stereotyping in her home, despite the fact that by her own account the females in the house did all the laundry, cooking, cleaning and dishwashing, while the males did all of the yard work, trash tending, and auto maintenance. So strong is the power of cultural conditioning, which insists each of us is completely master or mistress of our own fate, that we may be blind to evidence that contradicts our most cherished assumptions.

Still, for those who will push past a natural reluctance to admit to having experienced gender stereotyping, there is ample evidence that gender does play a huge role in shaping experiences and thinking. When the American Association of University Women (AAUW) published its groundbreaking report *Shortchanging Girls, Shortchanging America* (1991), journalist Peggy Orenstein set out to research its findings on her own, both in affluent and in poorer schools. Her work reinforces with great detail and sensitivity the overall findings of the AAUW, which finds that despite changes that have occurred in recent generations, many girls still experience "low self-image, self-doubt, and self-censorship of their creative and intellectual potential," and they often have lower expectations and less self confidence than boys. They also experience more depression and are "four times more likely to attempt suicide" (Orenstein 1994, xvi).

Like other researchers and writers, Orenstein traces these dismal findings to cultural conditioning regarding the "normal" characteristics and role of women. Characterizing American culture, she describes it as "ambivalent toward female achievement, proficiency, independence, and right to a full and equal life"; suggests that it "devalues both women and [such supposedly female qualities as] nurturance, cooperation, and intuition"; argues that it has taught women to undervalue themselves, deride their own abilities, denigrate their work, and discount their success. The results, she says, is that women:

> don't feel we have the right to our dreams, or, if we achieve them, we feel undeserving. . . . We learn to look outward for markers of acceptability and are particularly vulnerable to putting our self-esteem in the hands of lovers or husbands, to believing that only someone else's approval can confer worth. (xix–xx)

In short, women grow up thinking that they're best at nurturing others, at cooperating and being peace keepers; that they're probably not really very good at many things, even when they have a solid track record of successes; that they're more likely to experience failure than success, so they probably shouldn't reach too high; and, that the good opinion of others—especially male others—is critically important and the best measure of their worth.

That it will be natural for many readers to have trouble accepting these assertions is confirmed by the experience Orenstein herself reports as she researched her text:

> [T]here is another book I could write. It would be about how, in spite of all our success, in spite of the fact that we have attained the superficial ideal of womanhood held out to our generation, we feel unsure, insecure, inadequate. I resist applying this lens to my life, and I have tried hard to avoid it, to remain unseeing even when the

feelings it reveals threaten to overwhelm me. I wouldn't look through it at thirteen, when I lowered my hand in math class, never to raise it again, out of a sudden fear that I might answer incorrectly and be humiliated. I wouldn't look through it at sixteen when I winnowed forty pounds from my body, refusing food and binging on laxatives, eventually losing the ability to eat at all. I wouldn't see it when I declined to try out for my college newspaper, even though I dreamed of becoming a journalist. Nor would I see it at twenty-one, when I became paralyzed during the writing of my senior thesis, convinced that my fraudulence was about to be unmasked. Back then, I went to my adviser and told her of the fears that were choking me.

"You feel like an imposter?" she asked. "Don't worry about it. All smart women feel that way." (xvii–xviii)

However difficult women may find it to acknowledge the extent to which their thinking has been culturally influenced, there is a great deal of incontrovertible evidence that gender plays a crucial role in shaping thinking.

Because teaching has become women's work, the influence of assumptions regarding gender on women's thinking and behavior have inevitably shaped the teacher's role in schools. Although women greatly outnumber men in education, for example, power still resides predominantly in male hands. Commonly, elementary schools are staffed by females but headed by a male principal, a structure Tyack (1974) aptly dubbed a "pedagogical harem." Spring (1997) elaborates:

> Women were considered to be more effective in the education of young children because of their emotional nature and nurturing qualities, characteristics not ascribed to men. Men, on the other hand, were not considered ideal for teaching young children because of their supposed lack of emotional qualities and their reliance on the use of reason. The graded school with a single male principal in power and subordinate female teachers in self-contained classrooms fit nicely into these social stereotypes. From the perspective of nineteenth-century society, the rational male should govern the school and provide limits and order to the emotional nature of the female schoolteacher. (142)

While recent years have seen some change in this picture, the gender imbalance in positions of power remain.

Researchers Doud and Keller (1998) report statistical evidence that the "pedagogical harem" remains alive and well in contemporary public education. They found that in 1994, 65% of all principals were male. In elementary schools, where 84% of all teachers were female, only 31% of all principals were female. In high schools, where the number of female and male teachers were roughly even, only 14% of all principals were female. Even these figures show improvement from earlier years, indicating that while some progress is being made, it is moving at the proverbial speed of molasses.

As the rungs on the hierarchical ladder increase, the percentage of women drops even lower. In 1999, Keller reported the dismal representation of women in the highest ranks of school administration, the superintendency:

> Women constitute about 12 percent of the superintendents in the roughly 14,000 U.S. school districts. That's up from 2 percent in 1981 . . . but below the 75 percent of teaching jobs held by women and the 51 percent of the population that is female. Five years ago, I thought it would take another five years for women to take their place," said Paul D. Houston, the executive director of the American Association of School Administrators. "Now I think it will take another 10."

Women entering schools as teachers, especially elementary schools, tend to find themselves in a position where they are supervised—take orders from—men.

It seems clear that links to an earlier, more overtly patriarchal system are still embedded in the daily life of schools, even if current rhetoric echoes an outdated refrain "You've come a long way, baby." Power remains where it has been for a very long time, in the hands of men, and women are still very much expected to do as they're told. This bureaucratic reality is a source of great frustration for women who enter teaching specifically because they see teaching as an intellectually challenging activity that offers opportunity to help improve their students' future: "They are caught between the institution, which is not their own, and the desire to do important work with their own stamp on it" (Biklen 1995). Time and again, they are told to keep their "emotional" side in check and to follow the instructions provided to them by the more "rational" body of predominantly male administrators (and educational researchers) who dictate to them practices and policies that control their classroom activities. Females entering the profession will find that because of a gendered historical legacy, they will have far less freedom in their classrooms than they may anticipate. And, because they have been schooled to attend to pleasing others, they are likely to be more reluctant to speak out against policies and practices they personally find objectionable, sacrificing their professional voices because of a felt need to be peacekeepers.

Of course the gender stereotypes that play out in schools affect men as well, especially men who are interested in teaching in areas that have long been considered female territory, including pre-school, elementary school, and the arts. Like other teachers who consider teaching a way to effect change in the lives of their students, men who enter these areas often hope to counter prevailing gendered stereotype. Studying males enrolled in an early childhood teacher education program, Sumsion (2000) reports:

> These men welcomed the opportunity to 'counter sex stereotypes' (Guy) and to provide 'good male role models' for children (Michael). In particular, they were keen to challenge images of men as aggressive, powerful, unemotional and uni-dimensional.

They considered it vital for children to see 'that there are many different aspects of being male—a male isn't just the rough and tumble person . . . . I can show children that males have a sensitive side, and what we perceive of as being the feminine side' (Guy).

Men may pursue the education of young children, then, partly out of a desire to undo harmful cultural stereotypes.

However, when men are immersed in unfamiliar environments, especially those they interpret as being female, their cultural conditioning may lead them to betray their own intentions. The males in Sumsion's study, for example, reported being uncomfortable with what they perceived as such female elements of the environment as an apparent lack of emphasis on physical engagement. The researcher comments:

> Interactions between staff and children, for example, seemed characterized by physical passivity, which the participants interpreted as a feminine preference. Guy's overwhelming impression of a practicum with children aged from birth to three years, for instance, was of 'a lot of sitting around, giving hugs and cuddles and that sort of thing' [sic]. He would have much preferred more active 'rough and tumble' (and by implication, more 'masculine') physical involvement with children.

Men who enter classrooms with young children, then, are likely to find themselves influenced by gendered norms, whatever their original intentions. They face, however, even greater challenges.

The education of young children is so strongly conceptualized as a female profession that men may suffer from cultural suspicion about their intentions and/or their sexual orientation. The males in Sumsion's study, for example, report such effects:

> Far more detrimental [than discrimination by other staff] to these men's self-esteem was the constant need to counter community suspicion of men's motives for working in childcare. As James said: 'You seem to automatically jump to a position where you're continually defending yourself. It really wears away your self-esteem' [sic]. Several participants referred to experiencing self-doubt and guilt generated by this unrelenting suspicion. Michael explained how:
>
> > The boys are drawn to you, as a male and then you get girls who want to sit on your knee. And then you start to think . . . 'God do they [other adults] all think I'm a pervert because I'm bouncing this little girl on my knee? Why does that feeling of guilt come into your head? Why should it?' [sic]
>
> They found the need for constant self-monitoring depressing, as Guy explained: 'I've always got to be so wary about what I do and how I do it because of the way I might be perceived I find it so depressing' [sic]. For many, depression was accompanied by fear. James, for example, commented:

> I'm a fairly sensitive sort of person and I've become even more so, maybe even to
> the point of paranoia. I've always got it [the possibility of being falsely accused of
> child sexual abuse] in the back of my mind. The thought that somebody would ever
> think that I would ever do anything like that breaks my heart. (Sumsion 2000)

Men who take up work with young children routinely, and painfully, face such suspicion about their motives because of an implicit question in the situation: "Men
don't usually come here, why are you here? What do you want?" A second implicit
question is equally painful: "Or aren't you a *real* man?"

Layered on top of gender expectations are cultural expectations about sexual orientation: *normal*, the culture pretends, is *heterosexual*. Despite steadily increasing
evidence that homosexuality is a natural, biological disposition (Evidence 1993;
Holden 1992), prevailing norms insist on casting it as a perversion. As a result,
heterosexual men under the influence of cultural conditioning also suffer from suspicion about their own sexual orientation.

> Homophobia . . . works in insidious ways to reinforce dominant constructions of mas-
> culinity. The school curriculum is hegemonised and gendered. In high schools the tra-
> ditional academic curriculum occupies the upper rings of this hierarch, with the mas-
> culinised subjects of mathematics and science at the pinnacle. These latter subjects are
> the ones which are traditionally taught by men and which have the highest status
> within the school community. . . . Male teachers who work in the nontraditional areas
> such as home economics, dance, drama, early childhood studies or music or who teach
> in the lower grades at primary school are more likely to be subordinated within a
> school's social organisation of masculinity. Implicit in much of this subordination is
> that men working in these areas are not 'real men'. Such men are often typified or cari-
> catured as . . . soft, or feminised, males. Fears of this caricaturing may well lead to male
> teachers in these subject areas overplaying their masculinity in ways which reinforce
> those masculine practices which serve to oppress girls and women and those boys and
> men whose behaviour does not fit the I norm'. (Roulston & Mills 2000)

One male music teacher in the Roulston and Mills study, in fact, explicitly names
homophobia as a longstanding issue for him, when he discusses efforts to interest
boys in singing. He tells the class "Any guy who's worth anything sings," and says
in discussing the class's reaction:

> At first it was like 'What?' [laughter] But it confused them because their mentality of
> singers was, you know like, fairies sing . . . fairies sing and I said 'Are you calling me a
> fairy?' NO Mr. Howard sorry no no no' [laughter] because I sing. . . . oh I grew up
> with that . . . when I was in university we went and toured a lot of the high schools in
> the university choir and the most commonly asked question in high schools from us
> was 'Are you gay?' . . . you're male singers so then you're . . . a bit funny . . . that's a bit
> of [a] sore point with me. (Roulston & Mills 2000)

Like Whites who are unaware of their privileges until they must function as part of a racial minority, men who may have been unaware of gender influences may suddenly find themselves acutely aware of their masculinity when they enter a classroom considered the province of women.

The discomfort of straight teachers who fear that others will suspect them of being gay reflects the hostile environment for teachers who are gay. The homosexual teacher will often feel pressured to hide his or her sexual orientation because of extreme cultural pressure to conform to the norm, in effect feeling forced to live a lie. Gay teachers, even after award-winning work in schools, have been fired or threatened with job loss when their sexual orientation was made public (Rofes 2000; Dell'Angela 2000; Walsh 1998). Harassment after disclosure is common:

> More than once, I heard from parents that students of mine were mocked or derided by neighborhood children because they had a gay teacher. . . . I heard that our school's name (Fayerweather) had been transformed into "Fairy-weather" among the local children who attended public or parochial schools in the neighborhood. It hurt and bothered me that my charges—through no fault of their own—were often put in the position of being stigmatized or having to defend their teacher's sexual orientation, but I did not know if alternatives existed. When I arrived at school one Monday morning and saw the word faggot painted graffiti-like over the front of the three-story building, I could no longer avoid facing that what I saw as a civil rights issue—my right to teach children regardless of my sexual orientation—was experienced as a peer relationship or a safety issue for my students. (Rofes 2000)

For any teacher who cares deeply about the welfare of children and equally deeply about maintaining an authentic classroom identity, having a sexual orientation that doesn't happen to match the standard cultural template provides multiple conflicts and challenges. Attempting to reconcile the challenges often comes at huge personal cost and with little support. As recently as late 2002, the

> U.S. Supreme Court declined . . . to take up the appeal of an openly gay former teacher who claimed he was driven from his job, and into a nervous breakdown, by harassment from students and parents that his school failed to address. . . . [After the sixth grade teacher made his homosexuality known at a public meeting] some students began to call him "faggot" and suggested he had AIDS. He reported the incidents to administrators, but most of the harassment was anonymous and went unpunished.
>
> He asked that the district provide sensitivity training condemning such harassment, but administrators responded only with a memo urging teachers not to tolerate anti-gay taunts, according to court papers. . . . . [After transferring to another school, he] soon faced harassment from some parents and unknown others, including slashed tires on his car and accusations that he was a pedophile. He resigned in 1998, citing a nervous breakdown. (Walsh 2002)

The bias here, of course, reflects the significant amount of hostility to homosexuals present in American society writ large. In fact, a 1997 Gallup survey indicated that only 61 percent of respondents endorsed equal rights for gays teaching in high school, only 54 percent supported equal rights for gays teaching in elementary schools, and 33 percent believed that school boards should have the right to fire teachers known to be gay (Dell'Angela 2000).

Again, however much those who happen to fit the cultural norm may assume that their experience is typical of all others', those who enter teaching with any characteristics that differ from the norm find acute challenges to their long term success.

The Complexity of Cultural Conditioning

While it's clear that characteristics of race, gender and sexual orientation exert crucial influence in shaping life experience, two points in relation to the above discussion need to be made here. The first is that these factors are only among the most obvious and influences. Experience is also shaped by social class, native language, religion, parenting styles, and a world of other factors. In *Ways With Words* (1983), for example, Shirley Bryce Heath documented very specific ways in which religious expectations, community norms and parenting styles produced language habits and behaviors in children that caused them difficulty in schools. Children from one poor Appalachian community were judged dull by their teachers because they consistently quoted the Bible when asked to write "stories"; in that community, fiction was considered a lie and memorizing the Bible was a highly prized skill. In a second but culturally different poor Appalachian community, Heath found that teachers judged children uncooperative and belligerent because they exhibited assertive behaviors and language; in that community, the adult experience included overwhelming racial discrimination, and so adults taught children the assertive skills they considered necessary for survival in a hostile environment. White, middle-class teachers, having no understanding of the experiences that shaped the children in their classrooms, dismissed the children as either stupid or incorrigible when in fact they were neither. The point here is that if teachers are to understand themselves as well as their students, they will need not only to look at race, gender, and sexual orientation but also to consider a wide variety of other factors as well.

The second point readers must remember is that in relation to individual people, these influences cannot be neatly categorized as they have been here. Each factor is only one element of a personal kaleidoscope that makes each person who he or she is; when one factor, like gender, is layered upon another, like race, the kaleidoscope rotates and idiosyncratic experience and thinking result. For example, Black women have written a great deal about how their experience is different from that of White women. While both groups are affected by the cultural biases that apply to all women, Black women suffer racial bias as well, experiencing a sort of double whammy of discrimination. Hine and Thompson (1998) offer a useful overview:

> While black and white women share many concerns, they do not always have the same demons. Ask the average white woman what "liberation" means and she will probably talk about working outside the home because to her that means "meaningful" work. She may also mention developing confidence and self-esteem, especially when dealing with men. But those are simply not the goals of the average black woman. She almost certainly must work outside the home to support her family, as did her mother and her grandmother. And all too often their work has been anything but meaningful. She also has a confidence with regard to men that derives from her relative economic autonomy and from the history of male-female relationships in the black community. (quoted in Willis and Lewis, 1999)

The fact that no experience can be neatly characterized as "the female experience" or "the Black experience" does not mean that efforts to understand various influences are not worthwhile. Even a partial understanding helps us to remember that assumptions are a product of life experience, and therefore they will vary among people with significantly different backgrounds.

These are essential points for educators to remember. To be effective in classrooms, they have an obligation to do their best to understand how life experiences have shaped their thinking as well as that of their students. Only by recognizing and understanding the alternative perspectives born of widely different life circumstances can teachers consciously design ethical and appropriate professional practice.

For Further Reading

Dell-Angela, T. (2000). Gay educators discovering strength in honesty: Equal working rights don't always extend to the classroom a recent survey found [Electronic version]. *Chicago Tribune,* p. 1.1.

hooks, b. (2000). *Where we stand: Class matters.* New York: Routledge.

McIntosh, P. (1990). White privilege: Unpacking the invisible knapsack, *Independent School* (Vol. 49, pp. 31+).

Pailliotet, A. W. (1997). "I'm really quiet": A case study of an Asian, language minority preservice teacher's experiences. *Teaching and Teacher Education, 13*(7), 675–690.

Price, J. (1999). Schooling and racialized masculinities: The diploma, teacher, and peers on the lives of young, African American men. *Youth And Society, 31*(2), 224–263.

Quiocho, A., & Rios, F. (2000). The power of their presence: Minority group teachers and schooling. *Review of Educational Research, 70*(4), 485–528.

Roulston, K., & Mills, M. (2000). Male teachers in feminised teaching areas: Marching to the beat of the men's movement drums? *Oxford Review of Education, 26*(2), 221–238.

Singham, M. (1998). The canary in the mine. *Phi Delta Kappan, 80*(1), 8–15.

Weiss, D. (2002). Confronting White privilege. *Rethinking Schools Online, 16*(4). Available at http://www.rethinkingschools.org/archive/16_4/Conf164.shtml.

Wilder, M. (2000). Increasing African American teachers' presence in American schools: Voices of students who care. *Urban Education, 35*(2), 2-5-220.

Wise, T. (2002). Membership has its privileges. *Rethinking Schools Online, 16*(4). Available at http://www.rethinkingschools.org/archive/16_4/Memb164.shtml.

CHAPTER 3

Expanding Our Thinking: Learning about "Other People's Children"

The issues of color and class inequality in American society
are at the heart of the future of U.S. education.
RAY C. RIST

Let's hope that every teacher and future teacher would agree that everyone working in education wants the same thing: whatever is best for kids. The difficult question, of course, is what *is* "best for kids"—the question this text asks every reader to answer for him or herself after thoughtful deliberation. Chapter Two suggested that one preliminary part of this deliberation must be an examination of how any teacher's perspective has been colored by his or her personal background. This chapter suggests that another preliminary question for readers is "*Whose* 'kids' exactly are you thinking about?"

Given that the vast majority of teachers come from a middle-class, White background, it seems reasonable to speculate that many teachers actually have in mind kids who look and sound very much like them—which is to say, they may be thinking primarily in terms of middle-class White kids. And, in fact, there's a good bit of evidence that this is exactly the case. We know, for example, that relatively few White teachers are well-prepared to understand and effectively teach children whose background is different from their own (Cushner et al. 2000; Wolffe 1996; Zeichner, 1996; Banks, 1994). And, we also know that many teachers are unwilling to venture into schools unlike those they themselves attended:

> Many future teachers show a preference for teaching children whose backgrounds are
> similar to their own, perhaps assuming that they are ill prepared to teach other

people's children (Delpit, 1995). The literature on preparing teachers for diversity indicates reluctance by future teachers to work in urban schools serving students of color (Wolffe, 1996; Zeichner, 1996; Zimpher, 1989). Haberman (1994) points out that it is not by chance that 70% of the teacher education graduates in Wisconsin do not take jobs (p. 167), explaining that the available jobs are in urban settings where Wisconsin graduates do not want to work. Many of these teachers will spend at least part of their teaching careers in urban classrooms or with children of color. Not only will they find themselves in schools where they differ in language and culture from many of their students; they probably will differ in socioeconomic class as well. (Terrill & Mark, 2000).

Teacher educators nationwide are familiar with this phenomena of newly certified teachers opting not to teach at all instead of entering schools unlike those they themselves attended—which are often exactly the places they are most needed.

Since most of us are uncomfortable with the unfamiliar, and since we generally don't like to take on tasks we feel unprepared for, such aversion to working with unfamiliar children in unfamiliar settings in understandable. Still: it's a problem. *All* of America's children need good educational policies and good teachers; *all* teachers need to think about *all* children as they flesh out their own professional identities and as they develop personal stances on educational issues. To familiarize teachers with children who may not readily come to mind in general conversations about what's best for "kids," then, this chapter offers a brief survey of children who come from other than White, middle-class backgrounds.

Of course, as noted in Chapter Two, it is a mistake to over-generalize about any group. There is no single "middle-class, White" identity, and there is no adequate way to characterize "non-middle-class, White" children, whom Lisa Delpit has aptly described as "other people's children" (1995). By no means do all children of color, all poor children, all children who are non-native English speakers share a single, fixed identity. And of course, stereotypes of any kind are often unhelpful for classroom teachers who need to focus on individual children with unique needs and interests.

That said, however, it is still possible to paint various groups with sufficiently broad brush strokes (as Chapter Two describes those likely to enter the teaching profession) to offer useful food for thought. Whatever their individual differences, members of privileged mainstream groups—especially middle-class Whites—do commonly share a great deal of social power denied to members of marginalized groups who are commonly disadvantaged in a multitude of ways. So that teachers can be more inclusive when they think about which kids exactly they might be teaching in the future and what kinds of policies might make most sense for them, following is a sketch of the children and schools that are so often left out of thinking about "what's best for kids."

Who Are America's Schoolchildren?

Despite the tendency of teacher education students to conceive of schools as places inhabited by children who very much resemble them and their own classmates, the ethnicity and experiences of today's students are kaleidoscopic. A realistic picture of America's public schoolchildren is anything but affluent and White—a reality even the government is struggling to incorporate in its bureaucratic rituals.

> It used to be that students, at least in the official view of the federal government, were black, white, Hispanic, Asian, Pacific Islander, American Indian, or Alaska Native. No shades of gray, or any other color, for that matter. But new categories and a variety of racial and ethnic choices [for reporting data required by the *No Child Left Behind Act*] will give students 63 ways to describe their heritage—or allow them to choose none at all. (Davis 2002)

Together, the students of color and mixed heritage who will populate these various categories comprise a steadily increasing proportion of the school-age population. Even using older and fewer categories, figures from the 2000 Census embody the reality of growing demographic diversity:

> Hispanics and African-Americans are now virtually equal in number . . . The number of Americans of Hispanic origin jumped by 58 percent over the past decade, to 12.5 percent of the total population. African-Americans, including those who identified themselves as members of more than one race, climbed to 12.9 percent of the total, an increase of about 16 percent. Asian-Americans have almost doubled their presence since 1990, to 4.2 percent of the total population. (Reid 2001)

Schools reflect this growing diversity: 1 in every 4 schoolchildren is either Hispanic or African-American, and 1 in every three is a member of a racial and/or linguistic minority. While about 65 percent of today's school-age population remains non-Hispanic Whites, that percentage is predicted to drop to 56 percent by 2020 and to less than 50 percent by 2040, when a majority of schoolchildren will be members of groups now termed "minority"; only the states of Arkansas and Mississippi are not expected to increase minority enrollments significantly by 2015 (Olsen 2000b).

Some states, where urban centers are home to large concentrations of ethnic groups, already reflect this steadily advancing reality of a "minority" majority in schools. For example, in the nation's second-largest school district, Los Angeles, only some 10 percent of its 723,000 students are White and non-Hispanic, prompting a union official there to term California's cities overall "the new Ellis Islands of the U.S." (Reid 2001). On the East Coast, in Broward County, Florida, the nation's fifth-largest district, with nearly 242,000 students—young people come from at least 52 different countries and speak 52 different languages, ranging from Spanish and Haitian-Creole to Tagalog. The number of children identified as having limited fluency in English has nearly doubled since 1993–94, from 12,039 to 23,459. (Olsen 2000c)

Along with California and Florida, New York and Texas are also home to large concentrations of minority populations, and several other states are already experiencing the large shifts in demographics predicted. One Harvard researcher reports that between 1990 and 1997, the number of students with limited English proficiency (LEP) grew: in Alabama, by 429 percent; in Kansas, by 205 percent; in North Carolina, by 440 percent; and in Kentucky, by 208 percent. Additionally, in Omaha, Nebraska, LEP students grew from 500 in 1992 to 3,000 in the year 2000, reflecting not only a large Hispanic community but also a large number of civil war refugees from southern Sudan (Olsen 2000a).

When we talk about "America's schoolchildren," then, it's clear that we are talking about large numbers of students whose experience is not White and whose native language is not English. It's equally clear that the experience of these non-mainstream children is often not middle class.

Data from the Census Bureau indicate that in 1998, some 19 percent of children under 18—a total of 13.5 million children—were living in poverty, exceedingly modestly defined as $16,600 for a family of four ("Child Poverty" 2000). Among non-Hispanic Whites, 10.6 percent of children are growing up in poverty; among Asian and Pacific Islanders, 18 percent; among Hispanics, 34.4 percent; and among Blacks, 36.7 percent (Child Poverty 2000). In general, then, one in every 20 children comes from an impoverished background; for Hispanic and Black children, the ratio of those coming from poor homes is one in every three. Of course, these figures also mean that, contrary to many stereotypes regarding people of color, it is equally true that two out of every three Hispanic and Black children do *not* live in poverty. Like White children, children of color come from a wide variety of backgrounds. Yet, because poverty does unquestionably affect so many children, and especially children of color, it is important to at least be familiar with its dimensions.

While many believe that poverty is the hallmark of the lazy, of those unwilling to work, the reality is that

Since 1989, the number of children living in "working poor" families has grown dramatically. Those are families in which at least one parent works 50 or more weeks a year, but the household income is still below the poverty line. . . . [In 1998] about 5.8 million children lived in such households, up from 4.3 million in 1989. In 1997, nearly two-thirds of poor children under age 6 lived in families with at least one employed parent. (Olsen 2000a)

While politicians take comfort in statistics indicating that child poverty rates have declined since 1993, many educators are troubled not only by the number of working poor families by also by an increase in extreme poverty, concentrated largely in cities. As hard as it may be for many residents of comfortable middle-class communities to imagine, an analysis issued by the Brookings Institution, *Kids Count,* reports that

> In very high-poverty neighborhoods in central cities (in which more than 40 percent of households lived below the poverty line), 17 percent of households did not even have a telephone, and overwhelming majorities lacked the home computers and Internet access that middle-class children increasingly take for granted. (Olsen 2000a).

Lacking amenities including not only technology but often reading material like books, magazines and newspapers, children living in poor homes "arrive at the schoolhouse with serious deficits already in place" for these and a variety of other reasons (Chin & Newman 2002 6).

Poverty, Race, and Schoolchildren

Each of us is, in a variety of ways, privileged and/or disadvantaged by our own backgrounds. The experience of living in poverty, however much it may be romanticized in such cultural platitudes as "Money can't buy happiness," imposes upon poor children a formidable array of challenges to overcome. In a report of research studying the combined effects of recent changes in welfare regulations and high stakes testing for The Foundation for Child Development in New York City,[1] M. Chin and K. Newman (2002) report a distressing overview of such challenges:

> [S]egregation by race and income in schools has increased over the last decade, to the detriment of poor minority children. . . . [A] significant number of children arrive on the door of the kindergarten with significant gaps in "kid capital," the cultural knowledge that more advantaged children bring to the classroom as contextual understandings that make it much easier to move forward. Almost one-fifth (18%) are unfamiliar with the conventions of print: they do not know that English print is read from left to right and top to bottom or know where a story ends. Thirty-four percent cannot identify letters of the alphabet by name, which indicates that they are not yet at the first level of reading proficiency.
>
> Forty-two percent cannot count to 20 objects, or read more difficult single-digit numerals, and judge the relative lengths of several rod-like objects; though, most of these pupils (thirty-six percent) can count to 10 and read easier numerals. Six percent cannot count to 10 objects and identify simple numerals and shapes; which means they are not yet at the first level of mathematical proficiency.

The distribution of these deficiencies is hardly random. Age, gender and family background characteristics affect children's skills and knowledge. Children with below average skills entering kindergarten tend to have: a mother with less than a high school education (Zill 1996a); a family that received food stamps or cash welfare payments (Zill, Collins, West, & Germino-Hausken 1995); a single-parent as head of household (Dawson 1991; Entwisle & Alexander 1995; McLanahan & Sandefur 1994; Zill 1996b); and/or parents with a primary language other than English (Kao 1999; Rumberger & Larson 1998).

Children living in big cities (with populations over 250,000) were far more likely to have one or more of these risk factors (Zill & West 2000) as were kindergartners from minority backgrounds. Thirty-eight percent of Hispanic, 44% of Black, and 44% of Asian Kindergarten children had at least one risk factor as compared to 23% for Whites. Over 71% of the White children have no risk factors (Zill & West 2000: figure 9, page xxxii). These risk factors are predictive of school performance: nearly half of those with multiple risk factors score in the bottom quartile in early reading and mathematics skills and general knowledge. Hence it comes as little surprise that children who have one or more of these characteristics have difficulty in school (Pallas, Natriello, & McDill 1989). These findings are significant, because they indicate that the educational problems that children in poor families encounter are not simply a reflection of the schools they attend (Kozol 1991), but of the inequalities in parental and family resources that characterize them before they even get to the schoolhouse door. (4, 6–8)

Through no fault of their own, then, in the great race that begins when children enter the door of a school house, poor children begin at a significant disadvantage. And, two early reports on the recent developments suggest that poor children are likely to enter schools more disadvantaged than ever, despite claims that welfare reform stressing workforce entry would ultimately benefit children.

Beginning in the summer of 1998, researchers at The Growing Up in Poverty Project (sponsored by the University of California, Berkeley and Yale in collaboration with Mathematica Policy Research Inc. and the Manpower Demonstration Research Corporation) have been studying the experiences of single mothers with preschool-age children who entered new welfare programs. Its first report, while tentative and still leaving much to be investigated, is nevertheless discouraging, suggesting both that children are being placed in low-quality care and that the mothers themselves are experiencing significant depression—both factors with negative impact on their children's development:

Young children are moving into low-quality child care settings as their mothers move from welfare to work. This results in part from welfare reform, since single mothers must quickly find a child care provider, often without the financial aid to which they are legally entitled. Our observations of child care settings revealed quite low quality, on average. But low quality compared to what? Earlier national studies have revealed unevenness in the quality of centers and preschools located in middle class communities. Comparing our results to this earlier work, we find that children in the new welfare system have entered centers of even lower quality. Educational materials often are scarce, little reading or story telling was observed, and many children typically spend their days with an adult who has only a high school diploma. . . .

Most participating children were not placed in centers but in home-based care. By this we mean licensed family child care homes or individual kin members or friends (kith and kin), who now quality for child care vouchers worth up to $5,000 per year. These home-based providers fell below the average quality level of center-based programs. We observed fewer educational materials, much greater use of television and videos, and unclean facilities.

In short, we find that the welfare-to-work push on single mothers is placing a growing number of children in mediocre and disorganized child care settings. This represents a lost opportunity, for we also have learned in recent years how high quality child care can effectively boost early learning.(Growing Up in Poverty 3–4)

This study's findings relative to the home-based child care so often the only option for poor parents are also reported by a state agency in California: "the quality of home-based programs, including licensed FCCHs was unimpressive, and downright dismal in some cases" (Policy Analysis for California Education 2002, 1).

Lower quality care when parents enter the workforce is but one of the challenges outlined in the Growing Up in Poverty report. The low pay poor parents often receive when they enter the labor force is not only frequently insufficient to secure quality child care, but also too often it doesn't provide even base necessities; some 30% of Florida and California mothers studied reported that they "often or sometimes" had trouble buying enough food (6). Not surprisingly, given the multiple stresses of trying to raise children under harsh circumstances, researchers also determined that parents infrequently read with children and that the incidence of severe depression among mothers was as much as three times higher than the national average—both factors known to substantially delay a child's early learning (5). On the whole, tentative findings of this report detail that many very young and very poor children are likely to experience a variety of conditions likely to translate to escalating disadvantages when they formally enter the educational system, especially as their single parents are pushed into the workforce by welfare reform.

The Chin and Newman report of conditions in New York City (2002) similarly finds that conditions for poor children have recently gotten worse, not only for preschoolers but for school-age children as well, due in no small part to concurrent emphasis on welfare reform and on high stakes testing.

Low-income families are burdened by inadequate income (despite long work hours), irregular shifts, overcrowded schools, and uneven quality in after school care—pressures that more affluent, middle-class families are thankfully spared. Parents who are themselves poorly educated, low on literacy, and non-English speaking are not well positioned to assist their children in learning to read or mastering their multiplication tables. (Chin & Newman 2002, 3)

Moreover, when they enter school poor minority children "are more likely to go to school with other minorities, a high proportion of poor classmates, and be taught by less qualified teachers" (4).

Compounding the problems of New York families is a recent insistence by schools that parents take up the work of helping prepare their children for gate-keeping high stakes testing that now controls promotion in city schools.

[O]ne look at the brochures put out by the New York City Board of Education . . . makes clear how essential parents are to the task of pulling children over the hurdles imposed by high stakes tests. Parents were admonished to read to their children nightly, to listen to their children read back, to visit libraries and museum, to use trips to the grocery store as opportunities for problem solving in math. No longer was the homefront the place where kids relax and then do a little homework. It had become another site for test preparation with parents standing in for teachers after hours. Parents got the word that their children's future in school was at least, in part, their responsibility. And while this has always been true, the sense of urgency was underlined in missives that insisted that parents were being held accountable for their children's progress.

For middle-class parents long accustomed to this supporting role, the difficulties of "home schooling" are serious enough. Dual-career families are caught between the long hours at work and the ever-present responsibilities of parental tutoring in the evening. But affluent parents can trade on their own wells of educational advantage in providing that extra instruction and where that fails, they may hire tutors to assist their children. Academically oriented after-school programs are more likely to be in placed in well-heeled suburbs than in poor, inner city schools. Middle-class families are more likely to have reading materials in their homes. It takes little prompting for them to work with their children to learn letters, colors and numbers. They are, after all, the major audience for Sesame Street, originally developed to close the gap in pre-school preparation for poor children.

For poor parents, the task is more daunting, only in part because they lack the educational advantages and the material resources that can make a difference. What they did have, at least before they increased their work hours in response to welfare reform, was time. They could insert themselves in their children's schools as volunteers—and they did. They could find time and space in their cramped apartments for kids to do their homework—and they did that as well. Even when they could not tell whether the work was really done because of limited English proficiency, they could certainly figure out whether or not Juan was bent over his books. . . . Yet . . . staying on track, maintaining household discipline, attracting attention through volunteer work in school, and making time to go to the branch library, becomes much harder to do when work hours ratchet up. That is precisely what we observed during our fieldwork in 1998–99 as the consequences of the 1996 welfare legislation began to take root. (Chin & Newman 2002, 17–18).

Even as parents may themselves be poorly equipped to be tutors, they have often provided monitoring and support to their children intended to help them overcome educational disadvantages. Ironically, however, at the same time that such support is more important to schoolchildren than ever because of high stakes testing, parents have less—often no—time to continue their efforts because of recent welfare reforms that force parents out of the home and into the workforce, often for wages insufficient for food and quality care.

For the growing one-third of America's diverse and poor children, getting a good education is crucial to carving out a future in American society. Even though an education is unlikely to provide racial and ethnic minorities economic parity with the White mainstream (Hubler & Silverstein 1993), education does offer one of very few avenues of hope for advancement. However, until legislators and other authorities undertake more substantive and productive measures to reduce inequity, and unless we can educate effective and willing teachers to work with poor children, the disadvantages they suffer from a very early age are unlikely to be overcome—ever. Instead, teachers are too often unprepared to work with diverse student populations and so exacerbate existing problems:

> In a school culture that is passed on "by osmosis" to middleclass White children, minority children must try to cope with numerous cultural, ethnic, and/or linguistic differences between themselves and their teachers. The teachers often mistakenly attribute their struggle to lack of ability or motivation. (Groulx 2001)

A lack of understanding thus translates to misinterpretation—and to perpetuation of the very problems education is intended to solve.

It is imperative, then, for teachers to understand that the widespread poverty and general lack of education among non-mainstream groups are not evidence of dullness nor apathy, but instead are in large part a legacy of historical and pervasive discrimination and of current inequitable conditions.

Other People's Children: Educational History and Legacies

American schools have never done well by poor children, most often minorities. The historical experience of many non-White groups has been one of denial, segregation, and/or forced assimilation. For example, in the 1800s, after the federal government had seized much Native American land and segregated Native American peoples on reservations, it became widely accepted that it would be in the tribes' best interest to have children inculcated with the values and characteristics of White Americans. For many years, it was government policy to remove very young children from their homes and families on the reservations and to place them in boarding schools for a program of forced assimilation, an effort to turn them into what has been scathingly called "apples"—red on the outside and white on the inside. Lone Wolf, a Blackfoot, describes an experience typical for many of these children:

> School wasn't for me when I was a kid. I tried three of them and they were all bad. The first time was when I was about 8 years old. The soldiers came and rounded up as many of the Blackfeet children as they could. The government had decided we were to get White Man's education by force.
>
> It was very cold that day when we were loaded into the wagons. None of us wanted to go and our parents didn't want to let us go. Oh, we cried for this was the first time we were to be separated from our parents. I remember looking back at Na-tah-ki and she was crying too. Nobody waved as the wagons, escorted by the soldiers, took us toward the school at Fort Shaw. Once there our belongings were taken from us, even the little medicine bags our mothers had given us to protect us from harm. Everything was placed in a heap and set afire.
>
> Next was the long hair, the pride of all the Indians. The boys, one by one, would break down and cry when they saw their braids thrown on the floor. All of the buckskin clothes had to go and we had to put on the clothes of the White Man.
>
> If we thought that the days were bad, the nights were much worse. This was the time when real loneliness set in, for it was then we knew that we were all alone. Many boys ran away from the school because the treatment was so bad but most of them were caught and brought back by the police. We were told never to talk Indian and if we were caught, we got a strapping with a leather belt. (Nabokov 1991, 220)

Beatings, in fact, were common, and many children resorted to suicide as a means to escape lives they found unbearable. Not until 1969 with the issue of a report titled *Indian Education: A National Tragedy—A National Challenge* did the United States government acknowledge the harm done to native peoples with earlier educational policies.

Negative effects of earlier misguided policies linger on. Although many reservation schools have been established with the intention of rebuilding tribal cultural knowledge and pride, a legacy of social problems plague reservations (which many Americans do not even know still exist), and dropout rates for Native American students remain among the highest in the country. In fact, school retention is currently a high priority for the Bureau of Indian Affairs (Delisio 2001), which still is an active agency.

Mexican Americans, African Americans, and Asian Americans also share in a history of exclusion and segregation. Of course, slavery made education for African Americans illegal for many years, and afterward segregated schools legally provided

Black students with far inferior funding and facilities. Only in 1954 was segregation made illegal, when the famous Supreme Court decision in *Brown v. Board of Education of Topeka* found that "Separate educational facilities are inherently unequal." However, de facto segregation has continued in a wide variety of forms. For example, as recently as the 1990s cities like Buffalo, NY and Hartford, CT were still engaged in struggles to be released from court-imposed supervision following orders to desegregate (Hendrie 1998; Archer 1996).

Like African Americans, Mexican Americans and Asian Americans have also first been denied access to, and later segregated within, public schools. By the late 1800s, many Texas landowners were shifting from cattle ranching to farming, and new railroads also made it possible for Californians to ship agricultural products to the East. These trends created a need for cheap labor, and Mexicans were actively recruited to work in American agriculture. As Joel Spring summarizes,

> Farmers wanted to keep Mexican laborers ignorant as a means of assuring a continued inexpensive source of labor. As one Texas farmer stated, "Educating the Mexicans is educating them away from the job, away from the dirt." Reflecting the values of the farmers in his district, one Texas school superintendent explained, "You have doubtless heard that ignorance is bliss; it seems that is so when one has to transplant onions. . . . So you see it is up to the white population to keep the Mexican on his knees in an onion patch or in new ground. This does not mix very well with education." A school principal in Colorado stated, "never try to enforce compulsory attendance laws on the Mexicans. . . . The banks and the company will swear that the labor is needed and that the families need the money." (1994, 66–67)

A similar need for cheap labor had much to do with the experience of Chinese immigrants, 75,000 of whom were living in California in the late 1800s working in factories, on farms, and on railroads and suffering severe racial discrimination. The San Francisco school district refused to admit Chinese children at all, its Board of Supervisors issuing this statement:

> Guard well the doors of our public schools that they [the Chinese] do not enter. For however stern it might sound, it is but the enforcement of the law of self-preservation, the inculcation of the doctrine of true humanity and an integral part of the iron rule of right by which we hope presently to prove that we can justly and practically defend ourselves from this invasion of Mongolian barbarism. (cited in Spring 1994, 98)

When Japanese immigrants began arriving in the early twentieth century, they encountered the same segregationist policies. As is true for African Americans in many communities, Asian Americans continue their struggle against segregation and discriminatory practices in cities like San Francisco (Hoff 2003).

Puerto Rican children as well have suffered from historical insistence that the mainstream White culture of the United States is superior to any other culture. Although Puerto Rican students are often perceived as "foreigners," as "wanna be" Americans, the reality is that the tie between the countries is one that was originally forced upon Puerto Rico by the United States, which was granted independence from Spain in 1897, established its own government in 1898—and then lost its independence to invading U. S. military troops soon after. As the government did in the case of Native Americans, the government employed education as a tool to subjugate and "Americanize" the conquered Puerto Ricans. Schools in Puerto Rico were soon forced to have students pledge allegiance to the flag, to celebrate U.S. holidays, to study U.S. curricula and texts, and—most inflammatory of all—to provide all instruction only in English, an imposition that eventually failed miserably. Given this history, it is perhaps not surprising either that some distrust of U.S. government and institutions lingers in at least some Puerto Rican communities, as does an often tenacious insistence on the legitimacy of the Spanish language in schools and in other areas of public life.

Historically, then, populations *other* than the White mainstream have historically been treated as inferiors. In terms of education, this has most often meant either being denied education entirely or being segregated into inferior schools. For the subjugated Native American and Puerto Rican populations, it has also meant receiving an education designed specifically to eradicate their own culture, including their home languages, religions, and values, which the U.S. conquerors judged inferior to their own English language, predominantly Christian religion, and emphasis on competition and personal economic wealth.

Contemporary existing conditions cannot be divorced from these historical realities. Generations of young people have been denied the promise of American education to offer all children equal educational opportunity; generations of young people have listened to the stories of their family and community elders recounting U.S. government abuses they personally endured; generations of adults denied quality education have been unable to climb out of poverty. Of course, contemporary Americans are not directly responsible for the abuses of the past—but the fact that we are not responsible for the past does not mean we can ignore it, for at least two reasons.

First, the children in today's classrooms are often well-versed in these matters, and historical issues often help at least partly explain the resentment and resistance to educators—especially White educators—that many teachers encounter when working in racially diverse schools. For example, a White friend of mine had an enlightening experience a few years ago while teaching on the Navajo reservation. After she'd developed a positive relationship with one of her students—in part by asking him to help her learn the Navajo language—the boy played for her a tape on which one of his family members chanted, or sang, the tribal history of the Trail of Tears march, an important responsibility. While many Anglo teachers may not even know what the Trail of Tears was, my friend, like many others, worked daily in a classroom where that historical fact was a significant element of the awareness and perception of the students she faced.

In addition to lingering resentment and distrust, however, historical discrimination has a legacy of several very practical effects which do much to explain why "other people's children" so often fail to thrive in schools. Because they are likely to live in poverty, they are also likely to attend undefended and largely segregated inferior schools, and—not surprisingly—to achieve less academically than their White counterparts.

Other People's Children: Current Realities

The many disadvantages of growing up in poverty means that poor children generally enter schools with greater educational needs than their middle-class, often White, counterparts. However, with some few exceptions (Richard 2002), the norm is that poor children attend schools that are also poor, both in terms of their funding and the education they can and do provide—making a bad situation worse. As Deborah Meier notes, "The resource gap is shameful—whether we're talking personnel, technology, books or physical facilities" (Kozol et al. 2002). Evidence of what Meier calls "the resource gap" abound.

Richard (2002) describes disturbing inequalities in current funding based on a report from a Washington-based educational research organization:

> The wealthiest quarter of the nation's school districts on the whole receive nearly $1,000 more per pupil from state and local sources than the poorest quarter of districts—creating an educational "funding gap" . . . In many states, the report shows, the 25 percent of districts with the highest child-poverty rates receive less money per pupil than the quarter with the lowest rates of child poverty, based on figures from the U.S. Census Bureau. The report pegs New York state's funding gap as the nation's highest, at $2,152 per student, based on figures from the 1999–2000 school year. Illinois, Michigan, Montana, and Pennsylvania also had gaps exceeding $1,000, based on figures from the 1999–2000 school year.

As unsettling as these averages are, Jonathan Kozol has long been documenting the vast disparities among specific geographical communities:

> the children in poor rural schools in Mississippi and Ohio will continue to get education funded at less than $4,000 yearly and children in the South Bronx will get less

than $7,000, while children in the richest suburbs will continue to receive up to $18,000 yearly. (Kozol et al. 1997)

Simply in terms of equity, the difference in resources can be astounding when considered over time at the level of an individual child in an individual community. By one estimate, for example, "From birth to high school graduation, the average child in New York City will see about $25,975 less spent on his or her education than the average child elsewhere in the state" (Johnston & Viadero 2000).

The New York City gap becomes even more disturbing when it is viewed in the context of changing funding and demographics:

Up until the late 1960s, when white children in large numbers still attended New York City's public schools, spending levels tended to be fairly close to those of the surrounding counties. As late as 1970, in fact, when nearly four in ten schoolchildren in New York were white, the city spent a trifle more per pupil than was spent in Nassau County and adjoining Suffolk County on Long Island, and only about 5 percent below the levels in Westchester. Three decades later, with white student population having plunged to a surviving remnant of 14.5 percent, New York City's spending has collapsed to levels far below all three of these suburban counties. (Kozol 2002)

The situation of New York City schools is mirrored in many other urban districts, attended by large numbers of poor children of color; the trend is documented in a Harvard University research report that finds "Patterns of segregation [in schools] by race are strongly linked to segregation by poverty, and poverty concentrations are strongly linked to unequal opportunities and outcomes" (Frankenberg & Lee, 2002). Funding for public schools continues to rely primarily on real estate taxes which yield little for schools lacking wealthy landowners. School funding is, in fact, an issue of great political sensitivity, but taxpayers with the most funds have most political influence, and they—and so the politicians they support—have been reluctant to invest in any children other than their own. Calls for equity in funding have fallen on deaf political ears for decades.

In *Savage Inequalities* (1991), Jonathan Kozol describes in agonizing detail the decrepit, often dangerous schools that underfunding provides for poor children in a variety of urban areas, including East St. Louis, Chicago, and New York. Lisa Delpit sketches an apt snapshot of the kinds of schools Kozol details, describing them as

ramshackle buildings called schools, with faulty plumbing, malfunctioning heating systems, peeling paint and questionable electricity—reminiscent of the sharecropper shacks in Mississippi. Pizza Hut won't even deliver to the "dangerous communities" in which these schools are located. (Kozol et al. 1997)

Not surprisingly, certified teachers are no happier to be housed in such facilities than children, and so schools serving poor children are chronically plagued by a lack of qualified teachers. Children with the greatest needs, then, most often receive the fewest material and human resources, with the result, as Fruchter notes, that "As a nation, we get the schooling results we pay for" (Kozol et al. 1997).

The gap in achievement between non-White children—especially poor children of color—and middle-class White children is both well-documented and intransigent. Out of every 100 White kindergarten children, 30 go on to graduate from college, while only 16 of every 100 Black kindergarten children earn bachelor degrees; 34.1 percent of White students take college preparatory courses in 10th grade, while only 22.6 percent of Hispanic students and 25.7 percent of Black students do so (Borja 2001). Based on such trends, the educational prognosis for children of color is bleak:

> About 3.4 million students entered kindergarten in U.S. public schools last fall, and already, at the dawn of their educational careers, researchers foresee widely different futures for them.
>
> Whether they are white, black, Hispanic, Native American, or Asian-American will, to a large extent, predict their success in school, whether they go to college, and how much money they will earn as adults.
>
> By 2019, when they are 24 years old, current trends indicate that the white children who are now nearing the end of their first year in school will be twice as likely as their African-American classmates, and three times as likely as Hispanics, to have a college degree. (Johnston & Viadero 2000)

Of course, such significant and well-documented trends—which reflect disparities in achievement not only among poor students but among middle-class students in better funded schools as well—stem from a complex array of interrelated factors, and it would be unreasonable to suggest any simplistic cause and effect relationship between poverty and poor performance, and/or race. Still: there is no doubt that this "achievement gap" between White children and children of color, as reflected in "grades, test scores, course selection, and college completion" is real (Johnston & Viadero 2000) and that poor schools for poor children provide at least part of the explanation for why this is so:

> National studies by the Education Trust and other groups show that minority students, many of whom attend poor, urban schools, get poorer-quality instruction than their white or suburban counterparts. They . . . have less qualified teachers . . . and face harsher discipline when they violate school rules. . . . When teachers expect less of students, they get less—and that can skew standards from school to school. Data from the U.S. Department of Education suggest, for example, that an A student in a big-city school is achieving at about the same level as B and C students in suburban districts. (Johnstona & Viadero 2000)

Students of color are also disproportionately tested for and assigned to special education classes, a problem that one Harvard report links to "inappropriate practices in both general and special education classrooms [that] have resulted in overrepresentation, misclassification, and hardship for minority students, particularly black children" (Civil Rights Project 2002). The report draws strong and damning conclusions from its data, emphasizing the following in the original text with bold print:

> The research suggests that the observed racial, ethnic, and gender disparities are the result of many complex and interacting factors including: unconscious racial bias on the part of school authorities; large resource inequalities (such as the lack of high quality teachers) that run along lines of race and class; unjustifiable reliance on IQ and other evaluation tools; educators' inappropriate responses to the pressures of high-stakes testing; and power differentials between minority parents and school officials.

Low teacher expectations for minority students and a clear link to poor performance are, in fact, well documented problems (George 2002; *Reaching* 1999; Toch 1998; Delpit 1995).

Summary and Implications

This, then, is the history and current reality of American education for other people's children: deprivation; segregation; lack of resources, including such physical resources as a safe environment and adequate and appropriate learning materials and such human resources as well-qualified teachers with high expectations and intercultural sensitivity; overrepresentation in special education; and, to no one's surprise, an intransigent history of underachievement. Looking squarely at these realities, Lisa Delpit asks the questions that every educator interested not simply in the welfare of some children but in the welfare of *all* children must ask about the future of children of color: "Who cares? Who can protect them?" (Kozol et al. 1997).

To be sure, much has been written about the fate of these children, and there are many signs that a strong core of educators and others do genuinely care very much about them, although their efforts have been relatively ineffective to date. Instead, the many changes currently being implemented have come from others outside of the education community, conspicuously including national politicians who have been making a great deal of noise about how much they, too, care about poor children. Many educators, however, find their claims hollow. To familiarize readers with popular political rhetoric as well as its causes and effects, Chapters Four and Five will provide an overview of who exactly has been promoting recent educational reforms, why they've chosen particular strategies, and how well the many claims they make match certain realities that are rarely discussed.

Note

1. This research was generously supported by the Foundation for Child Development, the Ford Foundation, the National Science Foundation, the MacArthur Foundation Networks on Socio-Economic Status and Health, Successful Midlife Development and Inequality and Economic Performance.

For Further Reading

Agbenyega, S., & Jiggetts, J. (1999). Minority children and their over-representation in special education. *Education, 119*(4), 619–632.

Biddle, B. (1997). Foolishness, dangerous nonsense, and real correlates of state differences in achievement. *Phi Delta Kappan, 79*(1), 8–13.

Bullough, R. (2001). *Uncertain lives: Children of promise, teachers of hope.* New York: Teachers College Press.

Delpit, L. D. (1995). *Other people's children: Cultural conflict in the classroom.* New York: New Press.

Ehrenreich, B. (2001). *Nickel and dimed: On (not) getting by in boom-time America.* New York: Metropolitan Books.

Kozol, J. (1991). *Savage Inequalities.* New York: Crown.

Kozol, J. (2002). Malign neglect. *The Nation, 274,* 20–23.

Mencimer, S. (2002). Children left behind. *The American Prospect, 13*(23), 29–31.

Ogbu, J. (1990). Minority education in comparative perspective. *Journal of Negro Education, 59*(1), 45–57.

Rist, R. C. (2002). HER classic: Student social class and teacher expectations: The self-fulfilling prophecy in ghetto education. *Harvard Educational Review, 70*(3), 257–301.

Spring, J. (2000). *Deculturalization and the struggle for equality* (3rd ed.). New York: McGraw-Hill.

Sulentic, M. (2001). Black English in a place called Waterloo. *Multicultural Education, 8*(4), 24–30.

Terrill, M. M., & Mark, D. L. H. (2000). Preservice teachers' expectations for schools with children of color and second-language learners. *Journal of Teacher Education, 51*(2), 149.

PART II

Considering Destinations: Truth, Consequences, and the Critical Vision

The nature of our schools will not change as long as our schools continue to focus primarily on preparing students to become economically viable. As long as educators are held accountable to the standards demanded by corporate America to produce marketable assets so that these corporations can make vast profits, the emotional health and well-being of students will continue to be of secondary importance.

DAVID O. SOLMITZ

CHAPTER 4

In the Interest of Everyone But Kids: The Politics of Contemporary Educational Reform

The enormous public relations industry, from its origins early in this century, has been dedicated to the "control of the public mind," as business leaders described the task.

NOAM CHOMSKY

National politicians, especially presidents, have spoken so much about federal funding and initiatives for education in recent years that most people assume that the federal government has authority over public schools. This is, however, a misperception. While it's true that the federal government has been increasingly involved in educational policies in recent decades, in fact the Constitution delegates authority for education to the states, and federal involvement has intensified only in relatively recent history. For many years, states fiercely resisted any federal intrusion into educational policy, and the federal government itself was never particularly proactive regarding education, having countless other contentious issues to worry about. But over time, issues that were clearly of national importance, like desegregation and widespread poverty, created a push for federal intervention into education.

No matter how important an issue prompting federal intervention might be, however, and no matter how much a national candidate might promise sweeping educational reform, Constitutional restrictions mean that the federal government has no power to force specific educational policies on the states. Instead, what it can do, and does do, is to shape school policy by offering particular financial rewards and penalties tied to policies it wishes to encourage or discourage. Essentially, the federal government decides that x or y is important, and then gives schools funds to support *x* or *y,* and denies funds to schools that don't do whatever the federal government happens to want. Because public schools are primarily funded through local property taxes, and because many schools have far less money than they need, financial incentives most often produce the desired results. Thus, while the federal government may have no direct control over education, it can manage to control schools indirectly through its funding policies.

In recent decades, the federal government has become increasingly vocal about its interest in public education and increasingly active in controlling state policy. In the 1960s, federal involvement stemmed largely from the Civil Rights movement and the perceived need to support desegregation efforts and to use education as a lever to help lift people out of poverty. In more recent decades, while federal interest in schools has intensified and some of the political rhetoric about education as a route to prosperity still rings familiar, the motivation for federal involvement has shifted from concern for civil rights to concern for economic interests. To understand and assess recent reforms promoted by the federal government, it is necessary first to understand how these reforms have evolved, who exactly has been supporting—and opposing—them, and why both camps have assumed the stance they have.

Themes in National Political Rhetoric

Theme 1: Education as Workforce Preparation

Interestingly, despite ongoing and heated controversy around specific educational strategies in recent decades, and despite the fact that there have been both Republican and Democratic presidents in the White House, for some time rhetoric at the national level has reflected strong consensus about the primary purpose of public schools. At least since the 1980s, federal rhetoric as well as federal education initiatives and policies have been becoming increasingly aligned with what Chapter One described as "traditional" economic goals: "schools are expected not only to extol the merits of capitalism, but also to produce hard workers and energetic consumers." Whatever other issues might be publicly debated, and however the stance of particular politicians might differ on specific topics like vouchers, national political rhetoric has consistently assumed that the primary purpose of education is to prepare students for the workforce and for participation in a culture characterized by competition and consumerism. So ingrained are these ideas that no one even bothers to defend them, suggesting that each of these traits is simply a self-evident good.

Indeed, whenever each of our most recent presidents discussed their plans for educational policy, these themes of workforce preparation and engagement in a "global marketplace" have permeated political rhetoric. For example, Ronald Reagan commissioned and promoted a famous (or infamous, depending on your perspective) federal report on public education titled *A Nation at Risk* (which will be further discussed below). The report raised alarms among the public by citing what it believed to be the failures of public education in terms of a national crisis. Rhetoric of the report simply takes for granted the idea that the central goal of education is to produce workers willing and able to help the United States maintain its political and economic global dominance:

> The time is long past when America's destiny was assured simply by an abundance of natural resources and inexhaustible human enthusiasm. . . . The world is indeed one global village. We live among determined, well-educated, and strongly motivated competitors. We compete with them for international standing and markets, not only with products but also with the ideas of our laboratories and neighborhood workshops. America's position in the world may once have been reasonably secure with only a few exceptionally well-trained men and women. It is no longer. . . . Knowledge, learning, information, and skilled intelligence are the new raw materials of international commerce and are today spreading throughout the world as vigorously as miracle drugs, synthetic fertilizers, and blue jeans did earlier. If only to keep and improve on the slim competitive edge we still retain in world markets, we must dedicate ourselves to the reform of our educational system. . . . (National Commission 1983)

When human learning is termed "the new raw materials of international commerce," there can be little doubt about the federal perspective on the purpose of public schooling: the purpose of schools is to prepare workers, whose purpose is to maintain America's dominance in a global, market-driven economy.

Similar statements have come from all of Reagan's successors. President George H. Bush, the self-described "education president," outlined several goals for education (known as *Goals 2000*) in his 1990 State of the Union message. In setting the context for these goals, his remarks made clear his assumption that, from a federal perspective, the primary purposes of education are to produce intelligent citizens and skilled workers of use to the economy. In this context, schools become a kind of factory and students become products; indeed, investing in education is made to sound very much the same thing as investing in factories themselves:

> Yes, we are going to invest in America. This administration is determined to encourage the creation of capital, capital of all kinds: physical capital—everything from our farms and factories to our workshops and production lines, all that is needed to produce and deliver quality goods and quality services; intellectual capital—the source of ideas that spark tomorrow's products; and of course our human capital—the talented work force that we'll need to compete in the global market.
> Let me tell you, if we ignore human capital, if we lose the spirit of American ingenuity, the spirit that is the hallmark of the American worker, that would be bad. The American worker is the most productive worker in the world.

Having set this context for federal policy, Bush then laid out several related goals for education, including having U.S. students rank "first in the world" in math and science and ensuring that every adult becomes "a skilled, literate worker and citizen." Commenting on his own goals, he restated his rationale for his plans to invest in education, as in other areas, to ensure America's continued economic dominance: "These investments will keep America competitive." Educated people then—like oil or wheat—become resources for the nation to use in maintaining dominance in the global marketplace.

It is particularly interesting to note that Bill Clinton, a Democrat who theoretically offered a significant change in leadership after twelve years of Republicans in the White House, talked about education in very much the same terms as the Reagan and Bush administrations. That is, Clinton also worked from the assumption that the purpose of public schools is to provide workers to fuel the American economy. When he outlined his plans in his 1994 State of the Union address, Clinton, like Bush, made clear links between education, the workforce, and the economic future of the country:

> Our *Goals 2000* proposal will empower individual school districts to experiment . . . as long as we measure every school by one high standard: Are our children learning what they need to know to compete and win in the global economy? . . . Our school to work initiative will for the first time link school to the world of work, providing at least one year of apprenticeship beyond high school. After all, most of the people we're counting on to build our economic future won't graduate from college.

Although he made some changes in Bush's *Goals 2000* plan, Clinton simply built on what had come before when he proposed his own education reform package as *Goals 2000: The Educate America Act.*

In fact, Susan Ohanian (2002) waxes eloquent on the obvious continuity between Republican and Democratic administrations in terms of linking public schools with corporate goals and leaders. Not only are schools to produce workers, but corporations are allowed to specify what kinds of workers they want and how exactly they should be trained:

> In 1989 President George Bush the Elder called for what Clinton later actualized: enlisting corporate CEOs to reform education. . . . By the time Congress passed President Clinton's *Goals 2000: Educate America Act* in March 1994, the infrastructure was already in place. Take a look at *Reinventing Education: Entrepreneurship in America's Public Schools,* by Louis Gerstner, Jr., CEO of IBM (with Roger Semerad, Denis Doyle, and William Johnston). The fact that it was published within a month of the passage of Goals 2000 is no coincidence. One of the noteworthy features of Goals 2000 is that Gerstner and his cronies got to name the problem and define the solution at the same time. They argued the need for choice, competition, and technology in the schools; they defined students as human capital and the teaching/learning

compact as a "protected monopoly" offering "goods and services." They described the relationship between teachers and the communities they serve as similar to that between "buyers and sellers." Gerstner and company talked about measuring school productivity "with unequivocal yardsticks." They spoke of the need for national tests and "absolute standards," insisting that schools must compare themselves to one another in the same way "Xerox, for example, compares itself to L. L. Bean for inventory control."

Not surprisingly, the trend for government to promote workforce education—and increasingly obviously to shape education policy to suit the wishes of corporate leaders—continued with the return of Republicans to the White House.

The second President Bush, George W., stated in his 2002 State of the Union Message: "When America works, America prospers; so my economic security plan can be summed up in one word: jobs. Good jobs begin with good schools." Like his father, George W. Bush talked a great deal about reforming education when he campaigned for office, and once elected, he persuaded Congress to endorse significant legislation designed to bring states in line with his wishes—which, as it happens, precisely reflect the wishes of Gerstner et al. summarized by Ohanian above. The cornerstone of his reform effort, which is currently driving education policy nationally and which includes the new state testing requirements (or "unequivocal yardsticks") discussed in Chapter One, is the *No Child Left Behind Act of 2001*. In a forward to his "blueprint" for this reform effort, the President sounded again the familiar theme of schools serving children by turning them into productive workers: "In a constantly changing world that is demanding increasingly complex skills from its workforce, children are literally being left behind" (2001). The "behind" of the legislation package appears, then, to refer not so much to some children falling behind others in terms of health, safety and opportunity (as discussed in Chapter Two), but in terms of failing to develop whatever workforce skills corporate America says are lacking.

Each of these presidents, whose terms essentially span the last quarter-century, has sounded the theme that the federal government has a compelling interest in schools because schools produce the workers necessary to the country's economic prosperity and global dominance. A second theme that has been evident in their rhetoric and used as a rationale for increasingly intrusive initiatives has been that the federal government *must* involve itself in education because America's public schools are failing miserably.

Theme 2: Education Is Failing

The idea that American children are falling "behind" is simply the newest iteration of the theme trumpeted in Reagan's 1983 *Nation at Risk* report. As is evident even from its title, the often-quoted Reagan report characterized American education as so poor as to be placing the future of the entire nation in jeopardy. Some passages, including the following, were quoted in a virtual hailstorm of media reports in the weeks and months following the report's release.

> Our Nation is at risk. Our once unchallenged preeminence in commerce, industry, science, and technological innovation is being overtaken by competitors throughout the world. This report is concerned with only one of the many causes and dimensions of the problem, but it is the one that undergirds American prosperity, security, and civility. We report to the American people that while we can take justifiable pride in what our schools and colleges have historically accomplished and contributed to the United States and the well-being of its people, the educational foundations of our society are presently being eroded by a rising tide of mediocrity that threatens our very future as a Nation and a people. What was unimaginable a generation ago has begun to occur—others are matching and surpassing our educational attainments.
>
> If an unfriendly foreign power had attempted to impose on America the mediocre educational performance that exists today, we might well have viewed it as an act of war. As it stands, we have allowed this to happen to ourselves. We have even squandered the gains in student achievement made in the wake of the Sputnik challenge. Moreover, we have dismantled essential support systems which helped make those gains possible. We have, in effect, been committing an act of unthinking, unilateral educational disarmament.
>
> Our society and its educational institutions seem to have lost sight of the basic purposes of schooling, and of the high expectations and disciplined effort needed to attain them. (National Commission Introduction)

Effects of the report carried on well after the initial uproar quieted down. Its findings continued to be discussed for years, and they are still considered central to the evolution of federal education policy in recent decades. In fact, the language of George W. Bush in presenting his *No Child Left Behind Proposal* in 2001 is just as damning of public schools as the language of the *Nation at Risk* report (and just as insistent that good schools are essential to the national economy):

> We must confront the scandal of illiteracy in America, seen most clearly in high-poverty schools, where nearly 70 percent of fourth graders are unable to read at a basic level. We must address the low standing of American test scores amongst industrialized nations in math and science, the very subjects most likely to affect our future competitiveness.

Bush's rhetoric here is typical not only in that it charges schools with failing, but that it appears to base those charges on specific and persuasive evidence from reliable measurements—instruments that can tell us exactly what percentage of which students have the ability to read at a "basic level," international tests of math and science performance, and other measurements like the SATs.

The persistence and pervasiveness of this negative picture of public schools has been noted by, among many others, *Washington Post* reporter Valerie Strauss, who observed in 2000 that "For nearly 20 years, business, political and academic leaders have been sounding this warning: American students are global underachievers in math and science, posing a serious threat to the competitiveness of the U.S. economy." Strauss further noted that the "alarm began ringing in earnest with the 1983 release of "A Nation at Risk" and that

> The warnings have continued nonstop. Just this month [December], with the release of results that showed U.S. eighth-graders lagging behind their peers in Singapore, Japan, South Korea and Taiwan on math and science tests, public officials and business executives said our country's future prosperity was at stake.

Researchers David Berliner and Bruce Biddle (1996) have also described the pervasive rhetoric about educational failure in recent decades in similar terms:

> In 1983, the United States government published A Nation at Risk, asserting that American industry and our leadership in the world were endangered because of our poor public school system and the ignorant students it was producing. Hundreds of similar reports followed. . . .

For decades now, the idea that public schools are failing miserably has saturated political rhetoric and been used to justify a variety of initiatives.

The overall message from the federal government has been clear: schools need to produce highly skilled workers to keep America dominant in the global marketplace, and they are doing a poor job in that area. Together, these ideas have provided the rationale for the increasing federal intervention in state educational policy, culminating most recently in George W. Bush's *No Child Left Behind Act,* which has resulted in statewide, high-stakes testing. Such federal initiatives have done much to change what is happening in American classrooms.

Because all educators assume a professional responsibility to advocate for whatever is in their students' best interests, much as lawyers and doctors have a responsibility to act always in their clients' best interests, it is essential for them to carefully examine these recent federal trends and to make an informed opinion about whether or not to support them. Since reform efforts rest primarily on the claim that public education is in crisis and needs federal intervention, the first step to thinking through the issue is to examine that claim. *Is* American public education on the whole actually in crisis?

This is, in fact, a question many people have been asking for some time, and their answer is a resounding "No, it's not." If this is so—if there is significant evidence that schools are actually performing well rather than poorly—then other important questions immediately follow: *why* have politicians in recent decades so consistently painted such a negative picture and argued so strenuously for strong (some would say draconian) federal intervention, especially specific types of interventions? •

Rhetoric and Realities

In the very title of her report, Strauss (2000) calls attention to the disconnect between the government's claims that the country is in economic peril and the strong economy of recent years: "When success doesn't add up—How can a 'Nation at Risk' continue to thrive when U.S. students score so poorly on math and science tests?" She asks,

> if our schools have been turning out dangerously ill-equipped graduates for two decades, why hasn't our economy suffered for it yet? How does one explain the last eight years of unprecedented economic growth, a period in which the United States became the envy of the world in technology, science and medicine?

Strauss is only one of many who have noted the discrepancy between the predicted imminent collapse of the American economy because of poorly educated workers and recent economic realities:

> Reagan's indictment of our schools as responsible for making us "A Nation at Risk" now seems laughable. Instead, we have built the world's strongest economy. American workers in manufacturing, service and agriculture attain the highest rates of productivity in the world. These achievements are the results of the creativity and work ethic of Reagan's hordes of mediocre school children. . . . Enough. The sky is not falling on America. (Berliner 2001)

If the sky is not in fact falling, why the constant cries of alarm? One of the people Strauss asked for an explanation was John N. Yochelson, president of the Council on Competitiveness, an organization that in 1999 issued yet another report warning that poor schooling was producing an inadequate workforce and threatening the American economy. Strauss reports that "'asked to explain why years of low math and science achievement by U.S. students haven't exacted a toll on the U.S. economy,'" Yochelson responded that he "'didn't have the answer.'"

Others who have been researching the hypothetical crisis do have answers, however. Among the most prominent of these researchers are David C. Berliner and Bruce J. Biddle, two respected and well-known researchers who have been working on these essential questions for some time. Their essential answer is, simply, that while *some* schools—notably those serving poor children—are in a deplorable state, the reality is that American public education on the whole is continuing to do an outstanding job despite an increasingly hostile and difficult climate. Berliner and Biddle summarize the findings of their research neatly in the title of their major work: *The Manufactured Crisis: Myths, Fraud, and the Attack on America's Public Schools* (1997). While the scope of this work cannot be adequately summarized here, it is important to understand that these researchers have gone to great lengths to scrutinize the evidence for claims about shortcomings in schools, and they have documented impressive evidence of their own that the scathing criticisms of schools in general constitute "myths" and "fraud."

Among the several myths that Berliner and Biddle discredit is that American students perform poorly on achievement tests, especially in math and science and especially in international comparisons. After a discussion of more than twenty pages in which they consider in great detail scores from a variety of recent standardized tests, the authors summarize their response to the notion that student achievement has fallen:

> Standardized tests provide *no evidence whatsoever* that supports the myth of a recent decline in the school achievement of the average American student. Achievement in mathematics has not declined—nor has that for science, English-language competency, or any other academic subject that we know of. Moreover, support for the myth of achievement decline has *always* been weak. Indeed, the two of us know of only *one* test, the SAT, that ever suggested such a decline . . . [but] the SAT is a voluntary test and each year is taken by differing types of students, which means that its aggregate results are not valid for judging the performance of American schools. Instead, the evidence suggests that average school achievement has either been stable or has increased modestly for a generation or more. And, although top-ranked students and those from "advantaged" homes have tended to hold their ground, those from "less advantaged" homes have recently shown achievement gains. (35)

As Mark Twain once claimed, there are lies and damned lies—and then there are statistics. As Berliner and Biddle show, statistics from various standardized, national tests have been misinterpreted and twisted to make them appear to support conclusions that they do not, in fact, support; they've been used to lie to the public.

The same is true of tests involving international comparisons. Again, the authors offer several pages of detailed analysis to refute the charge that American students lag behind other countries in educational achievement. In most cases, the authors find that conclusions are based on the kinds of faulty comparisons we generally refer to as "comparing apples and oranges"—comparing things that simply aren't comparable. The following analysis of one comparison is typical and clearly demonstrates the kinds of weaknesses Berliner and Biddle found in the evidence for claims that American students perform dismally.

> The Second International Mathematics Study from the IEA [International Association for the Evaluation of Educational Achievement] was conducted from 1980 to

1982. It looked at the achievement of both thirteen-year-olds (i.e., eighth-graders) and high school seniors. Among other things, the study found that the aggregate achievement of eighth-grade American students lagged behind that of students in many other countries, notably Japan. This fact was immediately pounced on by critics and by a dutiful press, which enthusiastically vilified American schools for fecklessness.

   Nobody at the time seemed to notice that Japanese schools were then *requiring* eighth-grade students to take mathematics courses that stressed algebra, whereas such courses were typically offered to American students a year or two later. However, this fact *was* noted by Ian Westbury, a scholar at the University of Illinois who knew the IEA study well. . . . Thus, what the critics had interpreted as a failure of American schools turned out to be merely a reflection of the age at which algebra instruction is typically begun in Japan and America. (55–56)

Comparisons must be carefully constructed and controlled, or the results are meaningless—or misleading. Unfortunately, the many damning comparisons of American students' performance are based on flawed comparisons that have been used to misrepresent a much more positive reality.

Interestingly, while many unfounded claims have been made about poor performance, much more reliable good news has rarely made it into public rhetoric about schools. For example, among several other bits of evidence, Berliner and Biddle report the following:

> In 1992 the IEA released a report of findings from a comparative study of reading achievement involving two hundred thousand students in thirty-one nations. In this study, American nine-year-olds placed second in the world—while our fourteen-year-olds finished ninth, which was well above average and only a few points off the top. According to Gerald Bracey, the IEA put out a major press release concerning the study—but not one newspaper, radio station, or television outlet in the United States chose to cover the announcement of this study and its results. Americans learned about it only after *European* newspapers reported it and some wire services had picked up the story of high American students' achievement in reading that had appeared in the European press. (59–61)

Among other good news that hasn't received much notice is the fact that Americans are "*far* more likely" to complete a college degree than others to whom they are so often compared. When one study reported both national and state comparative statistics on college graduation, the results indicated that

> More than half of all American states are graduating 27 percent or more of their twenty-two-year-olds, but the *highest* percentage for a foreign country (Japan) is 26 percent. Even the lowest-ranking American states—Nevada (with 13 percent) and Alaska (with 10 percent)—are graduating roughly the same proportion of twenty-two-year-olds as are major Western European nations that are so often touted as

models for American education to emulate. But have these data provoked noisy de-bate? They have not; indeed, as far as we can tell, media silence concerning them has been complete. (61)

Unlike the many critics of American education, Berliner and Biddle base their charge that poor school performance is a "manufactured crisis" on detailed, careful analysis of a host of complex factors. They offer compelling evidence that not only have reports of the failure of American public schools been as unsound as they have been pervasive, but contradictory evidence that schools are generally performing very well indeed have been ignored. And, as they also point out, the picture of the American worker as a poorly educated, unproductive drag on the economy has been discredited by a variety of factors, including a 1993 report that found "worker productivity in the United States had just hit a twenty-year high and was, as it had been for years, greatly ahead of worker productivity in countries that are our international rivals" (61).

None of this is to say that there are no problems in American education; to be sure, there are some severe problems, which will be discussed in later chapters. However, it is clear that on the whole American public schools are doing an outstanding job of educating their charges and are far from the dismal failure that many now accept they are. Given the kind of evidence Berliner and Biddle have presented, why have politicians—and others—continued to insist that schools are in crisis?

Why Produce a "Manufactured Crisis"?

The question of why such a dismal picture is painted of public schools in spite of their significant achievements is one that many people, especially many educators, have been asking for some time. The answers are disheartening—if, perhaps, not surprising in an environment where public figures take as a given that schools exist to serve not students themselves, but to serve and advance the American economy. Activist David Stratman (1997) makes a pointed and telling analogy:

> Since the publication of *A Nation at Risk* in 1983, there have been numerous reports issued, each declaring U.S. public education a disaster, and each proposing "solutions" to our problems. The sponsors of the many reports are a little like the conman in "The Music Man," who declares, "We've got trouble, right here in River City . . ." and the chorus repeats, "trouble, trouble, trouble, trouble . . ." He just happens to be selling the solution to all their troubles.

Indeed, every reported crisis has come been accompanied by particular reform strategies the federal government has wanted to impose (and often concurrently promoted by corporate America). As Stratman suggests, however, the public generally has its own ideas about what is best for its children, and so the first step to shaping public opinion to make it amenable to certain suggestions is to convince people that a terrible crisis is at hand:

> How do you sell radical changes that would have been completely unacceptable to the public a decade or two ago? You tell people over and over that their institutions have failed, and that only the solutions you are peddling offer any way out of their "troubles."

In other words, since most people would agree that "If it ain't broke, don't fix it," then change requires persuading people that the system is indeed "broke."

While the public generally feels it freely makes its own decisions, in fact the government historically has been in the business of consciously orchestrating public opinion. This is an idea that will be alien and unbelievable to many, and yet certain segments of the country have always felt that they have both a right and a need to control the opinion of the masses. Noam Chomsky (1999) demonstrates that many public figures, notably including such American giants as James Madison and Woodrow Wilson, were blunt about what they perceived as a need for an elite in a democracy to control public opinion. So widely accepted has this idea been that one prominent public relations figure who wrote about it in the most direct of terms was honored by a major American organization in the mid-twentieth century:

> . . . the doctrines that have been crafted to impose the modern forms of political democracy . . . are expressed quite accurately in an important manual of the public relations industry by one of its leading figures, Edward Bernays. He opens by observing that "the conscious and intelligent manipulation of the organized habits and opinions of the masses is an important element in democratic society." To carry out this essential task, "the intelligent minorities must make use of propaganda continuously and systematically," because they alone "understand the mental processes and social patterns of the masses" and can "pull the wires which control the public mind." Therefore, our "society has consented to permit free competition to be organized by leadership and propaganda," another case of "consent without consent." Propaganda provides the leadership with a mechanism "to mold the mind of the masses" so that "they will throw their newly gained strength in the desired direction." The leadership can "regiment the public mind every bit as much as an army regiments the bodies of its soldiers." This process of "engineering consent" is the very "essence of the democratic process," Bernays wrote shortly before he was honored for his contributions by the American Psychological Association in 1949. (53)

However repugnant many readers will find the idea that the government (and others) may be consciously manipulating their thinking, among many leaders such manipulation is perceived as a necessary and proper activity.

It is just such manipulation that Berliner and Biddle identified as they analyzed the evidence behind claims that public education is in decline. Both authors report that as negative pictures of public schools kept appearing in the press, they independently began to develop a sense that "something was not quite right, that organized malevolence might actually be underway." When they eventually joined forces to take a close look at the purported evidence behind claims of crisis, their worst suspicions were confirmed, and they say of their book that it was "written in outrage" because

> The more we poked into our story, the more nasty lies about education we unearthed; the more we learned about how government officials and their allies were ignoring, suppressing, and distorting evidence; and the more we discovered how Americans were being misled about schools and their accomplishments. (xiv–xv)

Exploring the causes for such distortion and manipulation, the authors found some contributors to the problem to be innocent of manipulative intent, but they also found many others guilty of actions the public would surely condemn were they to understand what has been happening:

> Some of those who have accepted hostile myths about education have been genuinely worried about our schools, some have misunderstood evidence, some have been duped, and some have had other understandable reasons for their actions. But many of the myths seem also to have been told by powerful people who—despite their protestations—were pursuing a political agenda designed to weaken the nation's public schools, redistribute support for those schools so that privileged students are favored over needy students, or even abolish those schools altogether. To this end they have been prepared to tell lies, suppress evidence, scapegoat educators, and sow endless confusion. We consider this conduct particularly despicable. (xv)

No doubt so will many members of the public and profession when they better understand whose interests exactly are served by the "manufactured crisis."

Corporations on the Crisis Bandwagon

Given the close ties between the theme of education as the production of human capital, of a highly skilled workforce, it is not surprising that business leaders have been standing alongside politicians bemoaning the state of schools, predicting imminent economic disaster, and calling for major educational reforms. As in the political arena, however, when the rhetoric of the leadership is examined in the light of economic realities, certain discrepancies arise that make the motivations of the corporate community suspect—at best.

The most obvious link between politicians and corporate leaders—who people the ranks of the wealthy and powerful elite—is that few people with aspirations to national office have the vast sums of money now required to run an effective campaign, and so those who want office must form alliances with those who can contribute heavily to political campaigns. Thus, favors go back and forth between the political and corporate communities as do individual people, who often move between government positions and highly lucrative jobs and partnerships in the business sector. Lamar Alexander, Secretary of Education under the first President Bush and former governor of Tennessee, is a typical example. Before becoming Secretary of Education, Alexander had extensive business dealings with Christopher Whittle, who created the commercial saturated Channel One television system now in place in thousands of schools and who has since founded the for-profit Edison schools. In fact, so obvious were the links between Alexander's earlier political posts and some of his very profitable business activities that during confirmation hearings, the Senate inquired carefully into them (Pound & Stout 1991).

Currently, Alexander is chairing a group known as The Council for Corporate and School Partnerships, whose members also include former U.S. Secretary of Education Richard Riley. This group seeks to promote active partnerships between corporations and schools, arguing—like so many politicians—that there is a critical "link between good schools, student achievement, and a prosperous economy" (Engeln 2003). Interestingly, the council also notes that such partnerships are likely to involve opportunities for corporations to advance "product sales" and "direct and indirect advertising"—more on that shortly.

However, the strongest link between corporate titans and political leaders is perhaps most evident in the workings of an organization known as The Business Roundtable, which has become increasingly influential since its founding a decade prior to the release of *A Nation at Risk:*

> The Business Roundtable, formed in 1972, is a coalition of CEOs of the nation's largest corporations. Now consisting of about two hundred CEOs, the Business Roundtable member companies employ about ten million U.S. workers. Over the last decade, it has positioned itself to turn its agenda for education into public policy, at both the state and national levels. It has entered into partnerships with state departments of education, and its members sit on national "advisory" committees. Most recently, Edward B. Rust, Jr., CEO of State Farm Insurance Companies, and Norman R. Augustine, former CEO of Lockheed-Martin, have been appointed to President Bush's education advisory committee. Rust is the current chair of the Education Task Force of the Business Roundtable, and Augustine is its previous chair. (Altwerger et al. 2002)

Still other links between the president's policies and corporate America are evident in the person of Sandy Kress, a former presidential advisor described as "a key architect of the No Child Left Behind law" who is now working with the Business Roundtable (Olson 2003a).

In its own words, this group is devoted to "improving public policy"—that is, to influencing public policy in ways corporate America deems desirable (The Business Roundtable "Agenda"). According to the group's web site, the purpose of its Task Force on "Education and the Workforce" is to "improve education performance and workforce competitiveness in the U.S. with an emphasis on ensuring that American high school graduates are prepared to succeed in the global economy." Its priorities are listed as to:

- Promote standards-based education reform in states, with a focus on the policy changes needed to produce measurable results. In particular, assist states with implementation of the landmark No Child Left Behind Law.
- Support state business coalitions efforts to improve state education performance, Pre-K–16.
- Provide an effective voice for the business community on critical education and workforce policies that affect the labor supply needed for economic growth.

Given the number of personnel who move back and forth between government positions and the Roundtable—and given that the Roundtable members employ millions of American workers—it is not surprising that this representative corporate voice forms a harmonizing duet with government voices: the purpose of schools is to provide the "labor supply needed for economic growth." Its idea of what should be happening is apparently instantiated in the *No Child Left Behind* law, which it has consistently supported. Its statement on "K-12 Education Reform" also sounds the familiar theme that "Most people agree that our schools need to improve. But how?"

That, indeed, is the question: if schools must change, what changes are desirable? Again not surprisingly, given the close relationships between the political and corporate worlds, the federal government and corporate American have been in agreement on the answer to that question. Again and again, with one voice they have promoted the same reform initiatives. These initiatives—some of which have already been effectively rammed into place by George W. Bush's *No Child Left Behind* legislation—will be examined in detail in Chapter Five. Even before looking at those specifics, however, it's important to understand the impact of the links politicians have already managed to forge between schools and businesses and the impact that linkage has already had on America's public schools.

Corporations in the Schoolhouse

Decades of insistence that "The sky is falling" (schools are failing; the workforce is deteriorating; the economic health of the country is "at risk"; schools must produce better student "products" for corporate "consumers") have already had one effect desirable from the corporate perspective: corporations now have a pervasive presence in schools, where they are exerting tremendous influence. Not surprisingly, the results appear tremendously beneficial—to the corporations.

Business/school partnerships. Not only has the "manufactured crisis" rhetoric persuaded the public that businesses are a logical "partner" in education, but lack of sufficient public funds for education have reinforced such "partnerships" by casting corporations in the role of *saviors* of education. Many schools find themselves without adequate funds to operate on any sensible level, and so being forced to look to elsewhere for money, they are attracted to the deep pockets of corporations. The very real funding crisis facing many public schools is one that most Americans find difficult to believe for two reasons: first, schools are funded primarily through local property taxes and most middle-class taxpayers feel (and are) heavily burdened by the proportion of their earnings that go to taxes. Secondly, the same rhetoric that paints education as failing also paints it as generously funded, despite some harsh realities. One of the myths that Berliner and Biddle expose, in fact, is "America spends a lot more money on education than other countries":

> Some years ago critics began to claim that America was spending a lot more for public education than other Western countries, and this idea has since been repeated endlessly. . . . [During the presidency of George H. Bush, a chief economic advisor, Michael Boskin] was quoted as saying that we spend more per pupil than most of the other industrialized economies. Nor was this claim made by Boskin alone. Two former secretaries of education, Lauro Cavazos and Lamar Alexander, also claimed that America spends more on education than do our industrial rivals, Germany and Japan. And former Assistant Secretary of Education, Chester Finn, wrote in the *New York Times* that we "spend more per pupil than any other nation," an opinion echoed by John Sununu [then Bush's chief of staff].
>
> In 1990 two members of the Economic Policy Institute of Washington, D.C., Edit Rasell and Lawarence Mishel, decided to check out the truth of these claims. They found that, like former Budget Director David Stockman a decade earlier, the people who had issued these claims seem to have made up the numbers as they went along. . . .
>
> When it comes to primary and secondary education, the United States actually spends *less* than the *average* industrialized nation . . . [and ranked] only *ninth* among sixteen industrialized nations in per-pupil expenditures for grades K through 12,

spending 14 percent *less* than Germany, 30 percent *less* than Japan, and 51 percent *less* than Switzerland. . . .

When we compare ourselves with other industrialized nations, we find that in 1985 most of them spent a *greater* percentage of their per capita income on primary and secondary education than we did. If America were to come up to merely the *average* percentage of the other [comparative] industrialized nations spent on education, in 1985 we would have needed to spend about $20 billion *more* on K-through-12 education. (1997, 67–69)

While $20 billion certainly seems—and is—a great deal of money, Berliner and Biddle point out that in terms of other federal budget items, it equates to about 20 bombers.

The issue of funding will be explored in more depth in the next chapter, but it's important to note here that the public has been led to believe that schools already receive a great deal of money. The fact is, however, that support for schools has been steadily eroding, and so school officials have had little choice except to seek funding outside of public funds.

The following experience of a father in Boston provides a good snapshot of the way schools have been forced into greater and greater alliances with corporations:

> The most obvious change in our schools in recent years has been the increasingly visible intrusion of private corporations. Here's how it happened in Boston. In 1992 there were drastic budget cuts, bitterly opposed by hundreds of parents and teachers who came night after night to public hearings literally screaming (many with tears in their eyes) at the School Committee for destroying successful programs and slashing already inadequate budgets. Nobody could understand why the budgets were being cut. It seemed crazy. But the cuts had a purpose which later became more clear.
>
> Once the schools were made destitute, city politicians linked them to corporations in "Public/Private Partnerships." Last year when my son attended the Trotter Elementary school, one of its "partner" corporations, Reebok, held a school assembly at which the company praised itself for being competitive by hiring workers in the Mideast for lower than US wages. Reebok even gave a marketing survey to the children to fill out. When I complained to the principal, she was sympathetic, but lamented that the school needed the gym equipment that Reebok donated, so she felt she had to let Reebok do the assembly.
>
> The budget cuts forced principals to go begging to corporations and undermined their ability to resist the imposition of corporate values in the schools. (Spritzler 1998)·

Essentially, underfunded schools are being forced into corporate alliances, which often offer the corporations a variety of advantages, including product promotion, market research, and the advancement of corporate values.

While many might think advertising in schools a minor issue, it's certainly very big business. Advertisers who buy 30-second slots on the in-classroom Channel

One programs generate $100 million in revenue for the company (Boyles 2002).[1] Corporations are especially interested in developing consumer loyalty to a particular brand as early as possible, since it is known that brand loyalty is an important factor in selling products. The link is evident in a recent article titled "Don't Spare the Brand," in a trade publication titled *Brandweek:*

> The issue, of course, is money. Many schools are lured by corporate benefactors because they face fiscal crises at a time when federal tax cuts and beefed-up military spending are leaving little room in the budget for education. In the process, schools are increasingly becoming a prime battle ground for marketers in mature industries, such as computers, who are anxiously trying to plant their stakes ahead of competitors. (Applebaum 2003)

While some opposition to advertising in schools has been arising, one consultant notes flat out that the soft drink and snack industries, for example, are unlikely to be thrust out of schools anytime soon because "They make too much money from the vending machines and rely too much on that kind of advertising to establish early brand loyalty" (Applebaum 2003). And, as Applebaum notes, "Just what constitutes 'early,' is getting younger all the time," adding as an example that the Dole company recently began a brand promotion campaign to thousands of elementary school students.

Product peddling goes far beyond hallway and lunchroom drinks and snacks, however.

> Today's classroom is a battleground for marketers of everything from soft drinks to software. . . . In the public school district of Philadelphia, lunch menus are printed courtesy of the Cartoon Network. Along with the daily specials, they feature the Turner network's logo, characters and information regarding promotions on upcoming shows. At a middle school in Seattle, a history lesson on the Civil War comes packaged by Procter & Gamble, complete with sleek-looking visuals and a page titled "Did You Know?" that informs students, among other things, that P&G had provided soap supplies to the Union army.

So huge are the stakes that there is little in the way of promotion that seems unacceptable to advertisers. A few years ago, General Mills actually paid teachers a fee to allow an ad for one of its sugar cereals to be placed on their cars, which they were to park as close to schools buses as possible so that a maximum number of children would see the ads.

Products are not the only thing corporations are selling, however. As reported by the Boston parent in the anecdote above, once corporations are in schools, they have a captive audience for conducting marketing research, analyzing student behavior and thinking so that ads can be better tailored to ensure their success. For example,

Channel One, viewed by over 8 million students, provides a 12- to 15-minute newscast and review of current events adjusted for different age groups. This service, free for schools, is sponsored by advertisers—who pay. Feedback from students as to what designer labels they prefer and what advertising they enjoy seeing on TV is then sold as marketing data. (Buchen 1999)

Corporations spend billions on advertising to ensure they attract young consumers as early as possible, and to the extent that schools deliver consumers and subjects for market research, they offer corporations invaluable help in selling both products and brand loyalty. Thanks to this mania for selling, students in the Brooklawn Public School District in New Jersey now play basketball in a new gymnasium named ShopRite (Cox 2003), and many other cash-strapped schools are similarly selling naming rights to their buildings.

Many would argue that the increasing commercialization of the schoolhouse is relatively harmless, just a natural extension of "the way things are." Many others would agree with Giroux (1998), however, that

> It still comes as a shock when an increasing number of young people, when asked to provide a definition for democracy, answer by referring to "the freedom to buy and consume whatever they wish, without government restriction" (Wright, 1997, 182)

As corporate America moves into classrooms and school buildings and onto school buses and teachers' autos, the message to students is clear: "Buy. And buy more. Be loyal to specific brands. And don't let anyone get in the way of your desire to buy as much as possible of whatever you want."

Workforce preparation. In addition to looking to schools to help produce enthusiastic, insatiable consumers and to provide marketing data to assist that goal, corporations also look to public schools to train exactly the kind of workforce that best suits the corporate bottom line, as is evident in all the rhetoric about competition in the global marketplace. As "consumers" of educational "products," corporations have strong ideas about what kind of "product" they'd like to see, and their involvement with schools helps them influence that "product." As Boston parent John Spitzler (1998) notes,

> Corporations want our children to see their futures through a corporate lens—as employees who must constantly prove their competitive worth to their employer's bottom line. They want our children to think that success in life requires that they demonstrate that they can and will work harder, faster, more skillfully, and for less pay than other people just like themselves. The idea of working together for each other's well being . . . is one which the corporations want to eliminate from our children's minds. . . . [At a recent award ceremony the] Mayor declared, "I'm happy we're here

giving our children the tools they need to compete in the 21st century." This theme was repeated by other politicians. Surrounded by corporate banners, prizes with corporate logos, and politicians pounding home the "compete, compete, compete" mantra, we all got the point.

Twelve years of training aimed at competition certainly helps corporations to hire workers ready to embrace the ideal of "winning" at any cost. (The real costs of this attitude, especially in terms of ethics and worker security, are just starting to become evident in scandals like the 2002 Enron debacle.)

But job training goes beyond attitude, often combining values considered desirable with skills considered desirable. For example, the sort of partnership promoted by the Council for Corporate and School Partnerships commonly results in projects like this one, sponsored by United Airlines:

> Because the company believes that the future depends on well-informed people who understand the impact of world events, the company seeks to bring the issues of international business and the global economy into classrooms in a variety of ways. One major effort is the company's founding sponsorship of the Virtual Trade Mission (VTM), an educational partnership developed by the federal government, educators, and private enterprise to teach high school and middle-school students the importance of the United States' export economy. The program was piloted in five cities in 1996 and was rolled out to 30 cities in 1997–98. . . .
>
> By participating in a virtual trade mission, created with the use of multimedia technology, students acquire the skills and tools they need to participate, compete, and succeed in today's global marketplace. VTM students work on a case study, wrestling with the problem of selling goods to an international market. . . . Future activities will include United Airlines' sponsorship of an actual trade mission to bring a product to market outside the United States. (Otterbourg 1999)

Here, the corporation has moved beyond the kind of character education that promotes consumerism and competition and is implementing a specific kind of training in skills and information it finds desirable. It's clear that students exposed to this program are supposed to accept increased global trade as a highly desirable goal they should help pursue and to develop the skills that will benefit the corporations that employ them to help with that goal.

It's unnerving to compare this kind of activity with a tongue-in-cheek description of the school of the future with the intriguing article title "Everything I need to know about edbusfotainment, I learned from my kid." Speculating on the future, the author asks readers to

> Imagine a future in which children will take as much interest in business as they do in schoolyard fads; a time in which they'll be as obsessed by financial instruments as they are by musical instruments or the instruments of destruction to be found in

most video games. Imagine the dinner-table scene as brother and sister, mom and dad (or whatever configuration of youths and caregivers prevails in that particular household of the future) enthusiastically discuss such issues as currency exposure, mass customization, internet portals, and the true meaning of "business casual." It will be a world in which there exists no artificial boundaries between work and family, no disconnection between the "workplace self" and the "homeplace self." These children, in short, will get a remarkable headstart on the road to becoming the business leaders of tomorrow—our star corporate managers, top executives. . . . [lessons might include] ethical and behavior issues, such as Etiquette and the Cell Phone: Should You Call from the Stall? (Thomas 1999)

As extreme as this picture seems, in the few short years since Thomas' satire appeared, corporations have continued shoving schools in precisely these directions.

Of course, many well-intentioned people find workforce preparation a reasonable goal, and it is—within limits. But one large problem with the current situation is that when corporate agendas shape workforce preparation, the corporations ultimately benefit at the workers' expense. The result of schools providing the training that corporate America requests, as they did following the call in the 1970s for more scientists and engineers, is that businesses end up with a large pool of highly qualified workers whom they can then hire at the lowest possible wages. As Stratman (1997) notes:

> Far from having a shortage of trained personnel, there is now in fact a glut of scientists and engineers in the U.S. The *Boston Globe* reported on 3/17/97 that, "At a time when overall unemployment has fallen to around 5%, high-level scientists have been experiencing double-digit unemployment." The government estimates that America will have a surplus of over 1 million scientists and engineers by 2010, even if the present rate of production does not increase.

Berliner and Biddle (1997) cite an example documented by Richard Rothstein (1993, 23) of calls for schools to do a better job of educating workers clearly designed not to alleviate shortages of trained personnel but to keep expanding the pool of qualified job applicants so that wages can be held at the lowest possible level:

> Pacific Telesis Chairman Sam Ginn complained to a 1991 press conference that his company gave a seventh-grade-level reading test to 6,400 "operator" job applicants, and more than half failed, proof of the need to provide "workers with skills that will allow us to be competitive into the next century."
>
> But Ginn failed to mention that for the 2,700 who passed his test, there were only 700 openings, paying wages of less than $7.00 per hour. A more telling conclusion would have been that the schools provided PacTel with nearly four times the number of qualified operator-candidates it needed, even at low wages. If the company offered wages above the poverty line, even more successful test takers might have applied. (91)

While it's true that today's students will need to be employed tomorrow, it is clearly not in their best interest to be equipped with an array of skills they will be forced to peddle for minimal wages in a fiercely competitive job market.

Staging for Twenty-First Century Reforms

Recent decades of what can be called (at best) propaganda have created a climate in which politicians have finally been able to force certain reforms businesses had long considered desirable upon the school community; other reforms are well on their way to implementation. The public has been, in large measure, embracing these reforms as well as corporate intervention in education because they have been persuaded that tomorrow's prosperity—embodying their hopes for today's children—depends upon drastic intervention in failing schools. But public education in general, as Berliner and Biddle demonstrate, is *not* failing, and if the future of tomorrow's children is in danger, it is not because schools are not providing the majority of those children with a good education.

Since the basis for the current reform agenda is a hoax, a "manufactured crisis," then the impetus for reform initiatives must lie elsewhere: the whole system "ain't broke," but strong measures to "fix it" have been successfully promoted anyway. *Why?* Chapter Five takes up that question, exploring the specific reform strategies so insistently promoted by political and corporate leaders—as well as who benefits from them and at whose cost.

Note

1. Although this scholarly article may pose a bit of a challenge for some readers, it is worth reading in its entirety for a detailed analysis of the corporate motivation for and dismaying but likely consequences of Channel One implementation and ideology—crucial issues whose detailed exploration is beyond the scope of this text.

For Further Reading

Applebaum, M. (2003). Don't spare the brand. *Brandweek, 44*(10), 20–26.

Berliner, D. C., & Biddle, B. J. (1996). In defense of schools. *Vocational Education Journal, 71*(3), 36+.

Berliner, D. C., & Biddle, B. J. (1997). *The manufactured crisis: Myths, fraud, and the attack on America's public schools.* White Plains, NY: Longman.

Consumers Union. (1990). *Captive kids: A report on commercial pressures on kids at school.* Available at http://www.consumersunion.org/other/captivekids/.

Giroux, H. A. (1998). Education incorporated? *Educational Leadership, 56*(2), 12–17.

Miner, B. (2002). Business goes to school: The for-profit corporate drive to run public schools. *Multinational Monitor, 23*(1/2), 13–16.

Saltman, K. J. (2000). *Collateral damage: Corporatizing public schools—A threat to democracy.* New York: Rowman & Littlefield.

Stratman, D. (1997). *School reform and the attack on public education.* Keynote Address to the Massachusetts Association of School Superintendents Summer Institute.

Thomas, S. M. P. (1999). Everything I need to know about edbusfotainment, I learned from my kid. *The Journal for Quality and Participation, 22*(2), 41–43.

CHAPTER 5

Consequences of Contemporary Educational Reform: Winners and Losers

McGraw-Hill has in recent years hailed the success of its education division in improving profits, citing repeated victories in Texas as being important in those gains. For example, company documents say that profits for the division in 2000 increased by 12.5 percent, to $307.8 million, from the year before. The company said in a 2001 statement that SRA/McGraw-Hill had a "stellar year" in 2000, with its phonics-based reading programs capturing 37 percent of the $100 million spent on textbooks in Texas—when Bush was governor.

The company has ties with Bush. Bush tapped company officials to sit on his transition team before he took office: Harold McGraw III, who is chairman, president and chief executive officer of McGraw-Hill Cos., and company board member Edward Rust Jr.
VALERIE STRAUSS *in the* Washington Post, *September 10, 2002*

As noted in Chapter Four, corporate America has already benefited in a number of ways from its general, recent involvement in education, including the ability to market products and cultivate brand loyalty among even the youngest students, to conduct market research on schoolchildren, and to shape the attitudes and skills of tomorrow's workforce. These benefits have come simply from opening school doors to corporate entry and influence. The future relationship between corporations and schools is sure to be influenced still further by the specific reform initiatives government and business leaders have joined forces to impose on schools, with considerable success to date.

For years, and despite some differences in the shape of proposals and implementation, those initiatives have headed in two primary directions: a) implementing standards along with high-stakes testing, and b) channeling money away from the public school system via a variety of methods, including vouchers and other "school choice" proposals. Many of these initiatives fly in the face of research and of the passionate opposition of countless educators, who have lost many battles to keep public money in and corporate influence out of schools.

Struggles over federal policy have, in fact, resulted in a number of clear winners and losers. A close look at the effects and potential effects of national policy and strategy makes clear that the winners in every case have been and will continue to be corporations and the wealthy elite who run and profit from them. Losers have been far more numerous and are found far from the board rooms and lavish offices of the wealthy and powerful: students, especially poor students, and the dedicated teachers who have spent hard-working, conscientious careers promoting the ideals of social justice and genuine equal educational opportunity.

While much of the following discussion relates to policies implemented by President George W. Bush, it is important for readers to keep in mind that recent legislation represents a trend that began decades ago and that has continued through a quarter-century of both Republican and Democratic administrations. The agenda played out in current legislation is hardly Bush's alone, and examples taken from his administration should be considered just that—examples of the kinds of arrangements and initiatives that mainstream politicians have been engaging in for some time and are sure to continue long after the end of the Bush era.

Standards and High-Stakes Testing

For some time now, many of the voices promoting educational reform have been calling, with a great deal of success, for implementing standards—a specific curriculum spelling out exactly what every child is supposed to learn and for accompanying large-scale testing. Of course, various promoters have had various visions of what these initiatives might look like and how they might be implemented, but the actual policies that have emerged have been strikingly similar:

> In the last decade, 47 states have adopted new standards for student learning and most have created or adopted statewide testing systems as well. Some of these measure student learning through complex, open-ended performance assessments. Most rely primarily on the multiple-choice testing technology that has dominated large-scale U.S. assessments for nearly 50 years. (Darling-Hammond 2002)

As Darling-Hammond notes, many of the early calls for accountability imagined it as part of a comprehensive reform package that included such other elements as high quality professional development for teachers and an assessment system that took into account the complexity of the teaching/learning situation in various contexts. However, what has arisen instead is largely a system of standardized, multiple-choice tests used in what is known as a "high-stakes" testing situation, where results of a single test determine a variety of future events. Often, test scores determine promotion to the next grade, or tracking into a particular course of study—and most often, graduation. Poor test scores often mean that teachers and principals can be denied raises—or fired, and schools may lose funding or be entirely taken over by state authorities. Essentially, high-stakes systems work primarily through such threats as a consequence of poor test performance.

George W. Bush's *No Child Left Behind* (NCLB) initiative, which went into effect July 1, 2002, has cemented this trend into national policy by mandating that every state administer standardized tests to assess the progress of its students. Of course, because of Constitutional restrictions on federal power over education, the federal government cannot force this or any other specific policy on states. However, budget realities have given the initiative the force of law and "vastly increase[d] the federal government's role in education" (V. Strauss 2002b). To understand why states and schools are falling into line with the legislation, it is necessary to understand the current fiscal status of states and schools.

In short, states have been in severe budget crisis, facing "staggering budget deficits" (Fuller 2003); in 2003, estimates of total budget shortfalls ranged from $68 to $78.4 billion (Fuller 2003; Schabner 2003). Not surprisingly, state officials have had to curtail spending, including funding for schools. The 2003 shortfall in California, for example, led the governor to ask the legislature to approve $10 billion in budget cuts in the middle of the 2003 fiscal year, including revoking $1.7 billion that had been earmarked for school support (Fuller 2003).

Such cuts are exacerbating severe money problems that many schools have already been experiencing. Although the public seems largely unaware of the problem, the funding crisis for public schools has reached incredible proportions nationwide. The principal of one District of Columbia high school, for example, has been quoted as saying that her school is in such dire straits that it has stopped purchasing such necessities as toilet paper; the entire D.C. system has a shortfall of $63 million (Blair 2003). ABC news captured the reality for many schools in a report titled, appropriately, "Blood for Books":

> The parents of children at a Eugene, Ore., school who tried to raise $30,000 to save a teacher's job by selling their blood plasma may be an extreme case, but parents, educators, school administrators and activists across the country say that it is indicative of what public schools, and the communities they serve, are facing.
>
> "I don't want to say the house is on fire, but clearly states' budget problems and the proposed federal cuts pose an unprecedented problem," said Brenda Welburn of the National Association of State Boards of Education. "States have had problems before, but this is unprecedented because it is so pervasive across so many states." (Schabner 2003)

As a result of extreme and widespread state budget shortfalls, many states reported cutting core programs; 21 states reported cutting or freezing elements of their pre-K-12 curriculum (Schabner 2003).

The result of the state and school funding crises essentially erases the Constitutional intent to leave control of public schools in state and local hands. Yes, fiscally distressed states and schools can always "choose" not to comply with NCLB—"simply" by forfeiting federal funding for such programs as Head Start, intended for the benefit of the nation's poorest children. However, current financial realities have persuaded many state and school leaders that turning away from federal funding of any kind is simply not an option. Therefore, the testing mandated by NCLB has the force of law.

Of course, many hope that the testing initiative will have a positive impact. Like the idea of preparing students to find a job after they graduate (discussed in Chapter Four), the idea of setting high standards and goals and then doing testing to be sure students are meeting them has strong superficial appeal. Who would argue against setting high standards for student achievement and having an assessment system to make sure students are in fact meeting them? But as in the area of job preparation, the reality that results from actions based on this rationale is a far cry from the results the rhetoric promises. As with job training that benefits corporations by providing them with highly skilled workers forced to accept minimal wages, the implementation of high-stakes testing provides a wide variety of benefits to corporate America while simultaneously hurting students and teachers.

The Winners

As the quote that opened this chapter suggests, among the largest benefactors from the Bush initiative are corporate publishers of educational materials—sometimes very specific, very limited publishers, however, who have the kinds of ties to federal politicians discussed in Chapter Four. The most obvious example of how corporations benefit from widespread testing is the profit they make on the tests themselves. Most schools and states purchase standardized tests from major publishers, and testing is very big business indeed. Consider, for example, the profitability of the best-known testing corporation, Educational Testing Services (ETS), familiar to many people through its SAT (Scholastic Aptitude Test), widely used in college admissions processes.

While ETS has made much of its non-profit status, in 1996 it also launched a for-profit subsidiary called The Chauncey Group International, which could eventually assume the Praxis testing series that many states use for the certification of teachers. Even as a "non-profit" corporation, however, ETS certainly makes profits and disperses them in ways an unsuspecting public might not appreciate. For example, its 1995 tax return indicates revenues of $134 million for College Board and SAT products and $20 million in government grants among the $380 million income it reported (not including products that were handed off to Chauncey).

> These huge flows of cash, largely from the pockets of test-takers and taxpayers, subsidize a very generous salary structure and corporate lifestyle. ETS President Nancy Cole received total annual compensation of just under $339,000 plus use of the manor house on the former horse estate where the company is located in Lawrenceville, New Jersey. Vice President Robert Altman received even more salary and benefits, $358,000, but no housing allowance. Three other ETS officers broke the quarter million dollar a year level, and a total of 749 employees exceeded $50,000 annually. (Fair Test 1996)

Testing is already very big business and about to get much bigger.

Besides the increased demand for the production of standardized tests now required by federal law, there are signs that pre-tests for the mandated tests will produce a new market for still more tests. In New York City, for example, new testing requirements have proven a bonanza for one company that has long made money helping students prepare for the wide variety of test marketed by ETS. There, the Chancellor of schools mandated six tests *in addition to* annual state and city exams, hiring The Princeton Review company to develop the tests and to train teachers and administrators in how to use data to inform their efforts to help students perform better on the high-stakes tests (Herszenhorn 2003). New York City students thus will be subjected not only to a number of high-stakes tests, but a number of pre-tests designed to help in test preparation.

The Princeton Review is one of several companies for whom test preparation is a lucrative business—companies clearly among those who will profit handsomely from NCLB testing. John Katzman, founder of The Princeton Review, describes the general expansion that the push for standardized tests has accomplished in his company:

> The third division, K-12 Services, is our newest, about three years old. Over the past six years virtually every state has created state-wide tests for students from third grade to high school. These tests can have serious consequences for kids. If you don't do well you might have to go to summer school every year, you might not get a diploma. But these tests are really aimed at the schools themselves—which are good, which are bad. The state ranks the schools, and this impacts on merit pay for teachers and tenure for principals. If your kids do well in New York, you get a $15,000 bonus, and if they do poorly, you're fired. So that's a sea change in education.
>
> Now, under President Bush's education bill, the states will be required to test every year, grades three to eight, math and English. We set up this division to help

schools deal with tests in smart ways. If we can help schools, very inexpensively—at $5 to $8 a student—to align their curricula to the state tests, monitor their kids through the years so we can see who's having trouble before it's a problem, and counsel the teachers on how to deal with these tests constructively, we can improve the schools and at the same time improve the scores. (Atcheson 2002)

Virtually anyone connected to the standardized testing business in any way has profited nicely from the trend—including four legal firms and several internal attorneys working for ETS, who earned a combined $4.8 million for, among other things, fighting against test-takers rights (Fair Test 1996). As this testing-watchdog organization notes, "No matter what the form, profit-making or technically not for profit, testing remains a very healthy industry, at least for those who work for it."

The profitability of testing becomes even more clear with a look at other for-profit industries. Many of the publishers of classroom materials are also in the testing business—which offers them the ability to test specifically on their own curricular products, capturing the lucrative testing and materials markets with one fell swoop. Lucy M. Calkins, founding director of the Reading and Writing Project at Columbia University's Teachers College, says of accountability efforts in the area of reading: "The thing that is really scary is how do you prove your reading program is a success? It's by kids doing well on the standardized tests made by the same publishers that wrote the teacher proof programs" (in V. Strauss 2002b).

In fact, the most direct beneficiaries of the NCLB Reading First program are a few select publishing companies. Reading First provides $5 billion over six years to advance the stated goal of ensuring that every child reads by the end of third grade. Despite the fact that the teaching of reading has been a fiercely debated topic among literacy educators for some time, the Bush government has implicitly endorsed what is known as a phonics approach. Interestingly, the emphasis is based on a report from the National Reading Panel appointed by Congress—or more accurately, on a *summary* of the report "largely produced by McGraw-Hill authors who write phonics-based materials, and critics say it does not represent the complete report" (V. Strauss 2002b).

Given the close relationship between George W. Bush and the prominence of McGraw-Hill representatives in his administration, it is not surprising that some researchers report

One corporation that is particularly happy over the direction that education is taking is McGraw-Hill. As the nation's largest manufacturer of K-12 classroom publications, and attaining a total sales figure in 1999 of four billion dollars (Business Wire, 2001), McGraw-Hill stands to profit immensely by anticipated skyrocketing textbook production and testing. Its phonics programs, Open Court and SRA Reading Mastery, are already mandated in certain states and school districts. (Coles, 2000)

In fact, the NCLB initiative is advancing McGraw-Hill's materials yet further, since its Open Court and Direct Instruction programs are among a very few programs that seem to qualify schools to receive funding from the Reading First monies.

One attendee at an early session intended to familiarize educators with the new Reading First initiative, Lisa Patel Stevens (2003), has written a detailed report of its events that make clear what direction the government intends reading teachers to take:

> Although an explicit definition of reading was not provided, commercial reading programs enjoyed an obvious and exalted status during the three days of the meetings. In the portion of the session entitled "Leadership," Phyllis Hunter (2002) advised the participants, through her speech, that their first and most critical role as leaders was to "fully implement a comprehensive research-based reading program." This single statement was repeated almost 10 times in the handouts provided to participants and voiced no fewer than a dozen times during Hunter's presentation alone. In fact, Hunter asked the participants to read aloud the sentence with her at the start of the presentation.
>
> In the portion of the meeting that was specifically entitled "Reading Programs," the focus of the context was primarily to show examples from "good programs and bad programs" (Eichelberger, 2002; Robinson, 2002). Although copies were not provided to participants due to copyright issues, examples from good programs displayed on the projection screen were those that used synthetic phonics approaches and included direct quotations, or a script, for teachers. . . . [T]he presentations that made up the bulk of the three days' meetings focused on reading programs. By name, Open Court and Direct Instruction were lauded through anecdotal stories provided by several of the speakers.

Conspicuously missing from this obvious endorsement, Stevens notes, was "discussion of the ethical consideration of seeming endorsements of Open Court and Direct Instruction by speakers, presenting on behalf of the U.S. government." Even more conspicuously missing was a discussion of the ties between George W. Bush and McGraw-Hill's CEO, who serves on the Education Task Force of the Business Roundtable.

So clear is the government's preference for specific commercial products that even the Association of American Publishers has sent a letter to the Secretary of Education indicating concern that some programs were receiving explicit preference (V. Strauss 2002b). The process by which federal preferences become state policy and deposits money in particular pockets has been made clear in Florida, which was among the first of three states to successfully apply for Reading First fund:

> This happened a few months after Gov. Jeb Bush, the president's brother, announced an unprecedented agreement with several major publishers to provide as much as 100 hours of free training to Florida's teachers. The offer is available to those districts that

purchase the publishers' products; Florida districts have $100 million to spend this year on "research-based" instructional materials. (V. Strauss 2002b)

Of the five publishers who signed on to this deal, two were McGraw-Hill companies (Macmillan/McGraw-Hill and SRA/McGraw-Hill).

Another state that has fallen into line with companies having ties to the Bush administration is New York, where state officials informed school officials that if they wanted Reading First money, they needed to use an online program being developed by a Texas-based company, Voyager Expanded Learning. Interestingly, Voyager's senior vice president Jim Nelson had earlier been appointed by then-governor George W. Bush as head of the Texas Education Agency and as head of the Texas State Board for Educator Certification. Later, Nelson was chair of a group called Education Leaders Council, a Washington, D.C. based reform group that supported the NCLB initiative. (V. Strauss 2002b)

So clear is the government's intent to promote certain products, in fact, that educators who have inquired into requirements for successful applications for Reading First money report that "With 'Reading First' a McCarthyist blacklist has emerged" and that the government-sanctioned materials are being endorsed as desired because so many school personnel "feel compelled to comply because educational funding is scarce" (Coles 2003). Clearly the Reading First initiative is accomplishing its own goals of promoting specific materials, generally being produced by corporations with close ties to the high level politicians.

The Losers

States. Just as the rhetoric about school performance is at odds with its reality, the rhetoric about financial support for the No Child Left Behind initiative has fallen short of the fine words and fanfare that accompanied its initiation:

> The web site of Democratic Congressman George Miller of California features a touching photo of the signing of the education reform bill at an Ohio school on January 8. Flanked by beaming African-American children, Miller, Democratic Senator Edward Kennedy of Massachusetts, and Republican Congressman John Boehner of Ohio—three of the bill's four authors—stand with Education Secretary Rod Paige in a happy barbershop quartet of bipartisan unity. George W. Bush, the self-proclaimed "education president," is also beaming, pen in hand, as he prepares to sign the historic No Child Left Behind Act of 2001.
>
> Just five weeks later, however, Bush wiped the smiles off those faces (at least the Democratic ones) by submitting his 2003 budget proposal, which came in $90 million shy of the commitments the education-reform act set forth. (Thrupkaew 2002)

Despite great fanfare about the legislation demonstrating a genuine commitment to improving education, details of the Bush budget reveal no substantive financial support for the cash-strapped public schools now forced to implement increasing testing and to buy federally-preferred curricular materials.

While Bush increased education funds by $4 billion, that is the smallest increase in seven years, constituting only a 2.8 percent increase at a time when increased education spending has averaged 13 percent; he has also eliminated over a $1 billion in funding to some 40 education programs, and so "as a result, 33,000 children will go without afterschool programs in 2003, and 25,000 will be deprived of bilingual education" (Thrupkaew 2002). Given the severe fiscal crises states and schools are currently experiencing, it is telling to note that while states project a shortfall of $68 billion in 2003, the top one percent of all taxpayers—those earning over $1 million annually—received a total $69 billion as a result of the Bush tax cut program (Fuller 2003). Bush's budget, in fact, allocated 59 percent of a $674 billion proposal to stimulate the economy to the richest 10 percent of all Americans while it concurrently cut state revenues by $4 billion (Fuller 2003).

The cost of all of Bush's testing—and the pre-tests that are coming into use to prepare for the required tests—is left to the states and schools to figure out for themselves.

Students. Students are paying for the NCLB initiative in a wide variety of ways: They are experiencing forced exposure to commercial programs that don't deliver on promises to improve students' reading abilities. They are being forced to take high-stakes exams that not only fail to deliver on promises to improve student learning, but also take a high toll in terms of anxiety and failure, especially for the most disadvantaged students. Simultaneously, students are subjected to classroom experiences focused on rote test preparation skills rather than genuine understanding. And, because of the way this particular deck has been stacked against them, many students will find their economic futures have been lost to the high-stakes test legislation.

Given that the Reading First promotion of commercial materials is being presented under the banner of "what works" and of constituting a "research-based" approach, like other mantras of political rhetoric, this claim is also a myth. While great claims have been made for the supposed "proven" effectiveness of phonics-based programs, especially of Open Court and Direct Instruction, researchers have repeatedly been trying to call attention to the fact that research to date does not in fact endorse those programs. Researcher Gerald Coles, for example, has produced an entire work (much like Berliner and Biddle's *Manufactured Crisis*) discrediting government claims about research support for reading programs aptly titled *Reading the Naked Truth: Literacy, Legislation, and Lies* (Heinemann, 2003). Coles finds the "research base" for these programs "a myth," as do many others.

For example, Stevens (2003) also points out that even if the summary of the National Reading Panel's report were accurate (which many writers have taken great pains to demonstrate it is not) there is still no support for the claim that there is scientific support for the government's preferred programs—all of which had production dates later than 2002.

> In fact, presenter Jo Robinson noted that "you can see that the publishers are starting to get it right now." If . . . the publishers are just now getting it "right," how can there possibly be scientifically based reading research to support these specific programs? To the contrary, the 30-year-old Direct Instruction program has been found to lead to decreasing comprehension scores in upper elementary grades.

While the rhetoric of reform keeps insisting that finally, educators are going to be forced into doing the right thing by children, the reality is that reforms are much more likely to benefit commercial interests than children themselves.

The same is true of the tests children are being forced to take. Given the enormous cost of high-stakes testing, one would think that it were a proven route to school improvement and performance. On the contrary, however, there is no evidence that it can or will work as promised:

> Accountability systems are being installed with frantic enthusiasm, yet there is no proof that they will improve education. In fact, to the extent that evidence does exist from previous rounds of high-stakes testing and extensive research on human motivation, there is every reason to believe that these systems will do more to harm the climate for teaching and learning than to help it. (Shepard 2002/2003)

There is, in fact, copious evidence that the tests will harm students in a number of significant ways.

On the simplest level, high-stakes testing creates an unhealthy, highly stressful climate for children themselves. The president of the California Association of School Psychologists has already reported, in fact, that children as well as school personnel are "nerve-wracked" over testing and that there are increasing reports of children becoming "physically and emotionally ill as a result of the new classroom climate" (S. Strauss 2002). Other researchers report that

> [t]here are increasing reports of students who become physically ill in anticipation of upcoming standardized tests. Alliance for Childhood (2001) has reported the "growing evidence that the pressure and anxiety associated with high-stakes testing is unhealthy for children—especially young children—and may undermine the development of positive social relationships and attitudes towards school and learning." (Altwerger et al. 2002)

This is hardly a surprising result since the stakes are so high and since, again despite political rhetoric, there is no evidence that a single test is an adequate or reliable measure of what children do and don't know. In fact, the American Psychological

Association, the American Educational Research Association, and the National Council on Measurement in Education have all been clear in stating that "test scores are too limited and unstable a measure to be used as the sole source of information for any major decision about student placement or promotion" (Darling-Hammond 2002).

In addition to the unreliability of a single score as a grounds to make major decisions about students' futures, the notion that every child can and will learn exactly the same thing in exactly the same way at exactly the same time is nothing less than educational nonsense.

> There is simply no body of accepted scientific knowledge that says that all students and all subgroups of students can reach meaningful high standards, at the required AYP ["adequate yearly progress"] pace, given the levels of funding and the lack of social, economic, and family assets of many of our children. It is also doubtful that the "machinery" will work. Indeed, there is scant evidence that the AYP train can even get out of the station. (Mathis 2003)

Expecting every eight-year-old to have experienced precisely the same mental growth at the same rate and level makes as much sense as expecting every one of them to fit perfectly inside size eight clothing—but that is nevertheless exactly what the tests demand. And, it is an idea that not only cannot be supported with empirical evidence, but one which has already been a demonstrable failure in earlier attempts.

Testing as the stick that will force all students through the same hoops at the same time has already been tried, with poor results. In the 1980s, for example, New York City had a program that retained students in 4th and 8th grade if they failed city reading and math tests. As a result, many students spent years in the same grade and "evaluations found that these students had lower achievement, greater incidences of disciplinary difficulties, and higher dropout rates. In 1988, the program was disbanded as a failure" (Darling-Hammond 2002). Moreover,

> Similar test-based accountability policies in Chicago, Los Angeles, and Atlanta, Georgia that led to large increases in grade retention and dropping out caused researchers to conclude that the net effects were negative for both students and the school system. (Darling-Hammond 2002).

The expectations for students, then, are unrealistic—especially so in terms of the poorest students who begin school, as Chapter Three discussed, already disadvantaged relative to their more affluent classmates.

Many argue, in fact, that the situation creates nearly inevitable failure for students from poor homes, and then adds insult to injury by blaming the students themselves for their failures.

[T]he mantra that all children can learn has been twisted into the belief that if they don't learn (pass the test) it must be their fault—an argument repeated by policy-makers on a regular basis. High stakes may make some students try harder, but do teachers (or politicians) really believe that the 6,000 Massachusetts students who have taken the MCAS five times, and similar students in other states, are not trying?

This is a blame-the-victim approach. It rationalizes leaving behind all the students who don't pass a test on the presumption they aren't trying, despite evidence that most are trying very hard indeed. And it ignores the fact that many students lack supports that are common in middle-class households—parents at home, lots of books, a quiet place to work—and that others face social, emotional, academic, or economic problems (for example, homelessness) or speak another language.

Standards require the most progress from students with the farthest to go. Without extra help and extra time, such a requirement may not be realistic or fair. Extra time is essential in a standards-based system, but new time-based schools have not emerged to replace our current age-based schools. Instead, some children are labeled failures through much of their schooling. (Gratz 2003)

Given the lack of funding for mandates as well as the severe fiscal crises states and schools are experiencing, there is no chance of students "with the farthest to go" getting the small classes, special attention and dedicated support that might allow them some hope of catching up and keeping up with their mainstream peers.

But even students who do pass the test may have gained little of value in doing so. While it is an article of faith that a single test score can offer definitive information about what a student does and doesn't know—despite several professional organizations' insistence that a single score is an unreliable indicator—there is also evidence that students can be schooled in passing tests at the cost of genuine learning and understanding:

One high-stakes test for third graders included a math item showing three ice cream cones. The directions said to "circle one-third of the ice cream cones." Correspondingly, the district practice materials included an item where students were to circle one-third of three umbrellas. But what we have learned from research is that many students who have practiced this item only this way cannot necessarily circle two-thirds of three ice cream cones, and most certainly cannot circle two-thirds of nine Popsicle sticks.

Other systematic studies show dramatically what students don't know when they learn only the test. In a randomized experiment conducted by Marilyn Koczer, students were trained exclusively to translate either Roman to Arabic numerals or Arabic to Roman. Then random halves of each group were tested on their knowledge using either the same order as their original training or the reverse order. Students who were tested in reverse order from how they had practiced, were worse off by 35 to 50 percentile points, suggesting that the high test performance for those tested in the same order as practiced does not necessarily reflect deep or flexible conceptual understanding. (Shepard 2002/2003)

Such experiences suggest that students who manage to pass the kinds of tests being implemented often learn little more than rote performance useful only in passing tests and offering little preparation for life after testing.

The heaviest impact of the tests are, of course, on students who don't pass them—a very large number of students who come from primarily poor homes. For example, a veteran Virginia teacher wrote:

> Hardly anyone . . . denies that a chief problem with the tests is that they favor higher-income and middle-class kids. Chris Gutierrez, who trains teachers throughout Northern Virginia in classroom techniques, says that kids who are raised in middle-class homes "will pick up most of the material on the English and history tests by osmosis. But for kids born in another country, the SOLs [Virginia's mandatory tests] can be unexpectedly difficult. Though all the research says that it takes 7 to 9 years to become really proficient in a foreign language, foreign-born kids in Virginia schools have to take SOLs after being here only one or two years."
>
> It galls Gutierrez that the state—and the media—laud the test scores of schools with overwhelmingly American-born and middle-class students, while condemning those of schools faced with the challenge of teaching large numbers of foreign-born and/or very poor children. . . .
>
> Understandably, administrators aren't too eager to talk about the breakdown of the scores by racial and ethnic subgroups as required by the "No Child Left Behind Act." Last year, 89 percent of Alexandria's white kids passed the Algebra I SOL, compared with 60 percent for blacks and 61 percent for Hispanics. In English, 94 percent of the whites passed, compared to 64 percent of the blacks and 73 percent of the Hispanics. (Welsh 2003)

In Indiana, failure rates have been 94% for Black students, 68% for Hispanic students, and 56% for students receiving free and reduced-price lunches (Mathis 2003).

Such inevitable failures triggered by unreasonable and unfunded expectations are already in evidence in many states, which are struggling with both practical and ethical implications of massive student failures. After a study suggested that at least 20 percent of California's students—including about 75 percent of students with disabilities and about half of all students with limited English skills—would not graduate in 2004 if the newly mandated exit exam were in place, the California board of education began considering postponing the deadline; in Massachusetts, confronted with the probability of vast failures among students with disabilities, its House of Representatives voted to allow some exceptions to its policy; in Florida, where more than 13,000 seniors were predicted to fail to earn diplomas based on the state's test, legislators passed a bill to permit students to use scores from other exams instead of the state test. The massive failures already occurring along with legislative backpeddling make clear the inappropriateness of the high-stakes strategy.

The disproportionate, negative effect on the nation's poorest students is one that many writers have commented on. It simply is not reasonable to expect that on the basis of threats and without extensive resources children with the most difficulties will suddenly be able to rise to some arbitrary—and questionable—standard:

> Once a child falls behind in school, it takes more than a "Texas miracle" for him to catch up. Research in literacy acquisition has been especially clear on this point. One of the most disturbing, if enlightening, findings in literacy research over the past 20 years holds that if a child begins school behind his classmates in rudimentary understandings of rhyme and letter sounds—the kind of knowledge that comes from having been raised in a literate environment—he will stay behind throughout his schooling. In literacy education circles, this is called the "Matthew effect"—the rich get richer, the poor get poorer. Most children who are identified in 1st grade as at risk for failing to learn to read live in poverty. . . .
>
> [W]e are creating, however unintentionally, a permanent underclass in our public schools—not unlike in our society at large. Many of these children *are* making progress in school, when we take into account the odds against them from the beginning of their schooling and the sheer amount of time it takes to make up a deficit in literacy acquisition. But increasingly, states are demanding that we not take those things into account. In fact, it appears that many legislatures have decided that the best way to deal with this underclass of children is to flunk it out. . . . No educator I know is opposed to "standards of learning." But high-stakes testing administered in this way, guarantees failure of the children I'm talking about. (Furr 2001)

And, not surprisingly, students who are flunking out are tempted to drop out; there is already evidence that eighth grade students forced to pass a promotion exam are more likely to drop out by tenth grade, and evidence that new high-stakes testing will exacerbate this is already appearing. As one *New York Times* article has reported, for example:

> Growing numbers of students—most of them struggling academically—are being pushed out of New York City's school system and classified under bureaucratic categories that hide their failure to graduate.
>
> Officially the city's dropout rate hovers around 20 percent. But critics say that if the students who are pushed out were included, that number could be 25 to 30 percent. . . . [E]xperts who have examined the statistics and administrators of high school equivalency programs say that the number of "pushouts" seems to be growing, with students shunted out at ever-younger ages.
>
> Those students represent the unintended consequence of the effort to hold schools accountable for raising standards: As students are being spurred to new levels of academic achievement and required to pass stringent Regents exams to get their high school diplomas, many schools are trying to get rid of those who may tarnish the schools' statistics by failing to graduate on time. Even though state law gives students

the right to stay in high school until they are 21, many students are being counseled, or even forced, to leave long before then.

And yesterday, after declining to comment on the issue for two months, Chancellor Joel I. Klein conceded the point. "The problem of what's happening to the students is a tragedy," he said, "It's not just a few instances, it's a real issue." (Lewin & Medina 2003)

Rather than helping ensure that struggling students get the support they need to be successful, the high-stakes system has actually encouraged schools to try and push them out of school, since their continued presence will continue to lower scores on the tests that have extreme consequences for schools and teachers. Again there is an enormous discrepancy between rhetoric and reality: if politicians and corporations are so sincerely concerned about the future of all of America's children, why impose a system likely to drive the neediest students out of schools and to fail others in vast numbers?

More and more educators believe that the corporate agenda driving the high-stakes testing movement involves long-term employment needs *not* for highly skilled and educated workers—which it is already getting in sufficient numbers to keep wages low—but for large numbers of workers who have been prepared to accept the most menial work for the lowest wages.

According to anti-corporate groups like New Democracy, headquartered in Boston where the Massachusetts Comprehensive Assessment System has spawned a student test boycott, the primary corporate goal is . . . to lower expectations about what education can provide. In this view, corporations are out to dim the hopes of students whose teachers might otherwise teach them they can get somewhere in life if they work hard and graduate.

The corporate problem is that educated people expect to get somewhere good. And despite all those high-tech job openings, there's even more of a need for low-tech service workers. Cooks. Domestics. Cashiers. Assemblers. Delivery drivers. This is the real new economy, where the job openings are, but it's not what today's students envision for their middle-class futures.

There's nothing more dissatisfied, and even revolutionary, than an educated work force that can only find low-paid jobs requiring low-level skills. People tend to accept poverty when they think there's no alternative, but not when they've followed the rules and still can't get ahead.

The corporate solution is simple: raise "standards" to arbitrary levels, assign impossible tasks and impossible tests, increase competition and stress, and make our kids think they're too stupid for anything better. . . . Standardized testing only ensures that more kids drop out into the lowest level of the service economy or into prison or welfare. (Fox 2000)

Here is where the most disadvantaged students are paying the greatest price: with their futures. What kind of job can high school dropouts expect, after all?

Whether or not one accepts the hypothesis that current conditions stem largely from a need to keep the vast majority of American youth anxious about obtaining even the lowest level work for the lowest wages, it's clear that the implementation of high-stakes testing—particularly without any funding to help the most disadvantaged students meet the goals—is hurting American public school students in a wide variety of ways.

Unhappily, their teachers and principals aren't faring any better.

Schools and teachers. One of the first and most obvious effects that high-stakes testing has had on schools and teachers is to push them toward the kind of unethical behavior demonstrated by pushing students who might lower test scores out of schools at earlier and earlier ages. With so much depending on testing results, educators feel forced to do "whatever it takes" to protect school scores. Getting the requisite number of students to pass the test has become a single overriding objective, with concern and support directed at those who can pass tests on time rather than on those who need more time or support. In Virginia, for example, where 70 percent of all students must pass the state's tests, a principal who was asked about the fate of the failing 30 percent responded "'It's cold-hearted . . . but I honestly can't afford to worry about it. My concern is the 70, making the 70" (Furr 2001). One teacher reports of another principal:

> The principal, in one of our staff meetings, said something like "Is there some way we could take these 20 kids, the ones who have no chance of passing, and send them on a field trip for the week?" She was just kidding, of course, but I think a lot of us were nodding like it wasn't such a bad idea. That's what it has done to us—made us so focused on our test results that we don't ask any more if it's right or not. (Perreault 2000)

With so much as stake, teachers and principals often feel they have no choice except to pursue the highest possible test scores, no matter the cost.

> There is evidence from studies in Georgia, South Carolina, New York, and Texas that high-stakes tests that reward or sanction schools based on average student scores can create incentives for pushing low scorers into special education, holding them back in the grades, and encouraging them to drop out so that schools' average scores will look better. (Darling-Hammond 2002)

Cheating on the tests in a variety of ways has also become "rampant" (Fox 2000). In addition to losing ground in terms of ethical behavior, teachers have also lost control of the curriculum, so that they can no longer teach what they believe in or what they believe their students most need. With that loss of control has come a concurrent loss of identity as professionals.

Teachers also reported that, as a direct result of state mandates, their schools had instituted policies about curriculum content. "We were told, 'If it ain't on the test, don't teach it.'" One principal told his teachers not to introduce new material in the six weeks before the test; this time was to be spent on review, especially in formats used in the upcoming exam.

"All [the principal] wants to know is how this relates to the objectives. It affects you, it really does. . . . [T]here's really not much enrichment." . . . Teachers noted that there was less essay work done, and that required writing often took the formats tested on state exams. "I think we're hurting the kids, honestly. I mean our scores are better but I just don't think they have the well-rounded skills they'll need." Other teachers noted the pressure they felt to keep on track with the prescribed curriculum.

"Before, you know, I could just go with the kids if something came up which hooked them. But now . . . I have to kind of rein them in. I know they get frustrated, and I sure do. I think, well, is this what I got into teaching for?" (Perrault 2000)

While many would applaud the fact that teachers are now all forced to stay focused solely on a mandated curriculum, that curriculum has been generally defined in the early grades as rote memorization of isolated facts and skills at the expense of more advanced and challenging learning experiences.

Other studies have also found that when teachers are forced to teach to test format they abandon instruction in such areas as writing, reading entire books, and long-term projects and instead emphasized such testing-popular topics as spelling (Shepard 2002/2003).

Teachers talked about feeling "defeated," "powerless," and "unsure if they were doing the right things" to help students succeed. . . . From the teachers' perspective this has negatively affected their sense of professionalism, decreasing autonomy and reducing options for children, but they do not see ways in which they can fight the trends. (Perreault 2000)

Between the constraints of preparing for tests and the promotion of commercially scripted programs, like the Open Court reading program being promoted via Reading First funds, control of the classroom is being taken entirely out of teachers' hands.

Here, again, is a conflict between rhetoric and reality. On the one hand, NCLB offers lip service to the importance of having a quality professional in every classroom. But again, the budget tells a different story:

Teachers, too, will have a hard time clearing the high bar the No Child Left Behind Act attempted to set. Recognizing that the quality of instruction has a significant impact on student achievement, the legislation requires schools to employ a "highly qualified" teacher in every classroom by 2005. But the budget freezes the teacher-quality program. In fact, as a result of the shortfall, 18,000 fewer teachers will receive training next year. (Thrupkaew 2002)

While everyone pontificates about the importance of teachers, then, there is no substantive support for teachers and schools to engage in the kinds of professional development efforts that would benefit the particular children in their particular schools. Instead, they are being forced to rely on training provided by publishers of products—as in the Florida example discussed above.

Adding insult to injury, there are moves to turn teacher "training" over to still more corporate influence. The trend for corporations to involve themselves with schools has now reached the point of shaping "training" appropriate teachers for their vision of appropriate schools:

> Louis V. Gerstner Jr., the former IBM head who co-chaired a prominent national effort to advance academic standards, has now turned his attention to better teaching. Mr. Gerstner is slated to announce this week, several weeks after stepping down as the chairman of the International Business Machines Corp., that he will lead a new, nonprofit group, the Teaching Commission. Organizers say it's aimed at formulating and promoting the best policies for raising teacher quality in the public schools. (Keller 2003)

While there are some few educators in the group, for some reason it apparently seemed to organizers that a corporate CEO would make a better leader for a group investigating what kind of teacher schools might need.

Interestingly, other members of the group include CEOs from 3M and Boeing and former first lady Barbara Bush; it also includes a former senior vice president of Edison schools, a pioneering for-profit school management company that will be discussed momentarily. Although the group is being funded privately, it "expects to make policy recommendations" within a year, "followed by a push to get them accepted" (Keller 2003). At the very least, events to date strongly suggest that whatever these recommendations are, they are likely to involve still more adherence to corporate values and wishes and still less autonomy for teachers in the classroom—both helping ensure that schools will continue to be what corporations want them to be in the future. The likely concurrent loss to teachers will be discussed below.

(A similar group, the Broad Center for Superintendents, has been founded to produce "chief executive officers" for urban schools, shaped as the Center—funded by private donations and founded by a former governor and the chairman of SunAmerica Corporation—thinks best. According to its website [http://www.broad center.org/gateway.shtml], "The Center's programs are particularly focused on identifying talented leaders from outside the field of education who have the passion, dedication and skill to take on executive leadership roles in urban education.")

All of the efforts to increase corporate influence in schools head in the direction of decreasing public and teacher influence and increasing private influence over what happens to children in schools. The other main thrust of recent reforms—privatization—is the goal towards which standards and high-stakes testing have been heading for some time.

Moves Toward Privatization

For some years, politicians have been pursuing a number of routes to turn control of public schools over to private, profit-making corporations. Common mechanisms here include "school choice" and "voucher" programs that allow states and local governments to channel public tax money into private schools. President Bush's proposed budget for 2004 is typical of the kinds of moves politicians have made in this area. It included both $75 million funding for a "choice incentive" and an income-tax credit up to $2,500 that applied to private schools (Robelen 2003). Such initiatives allow public tax money to be taken out of already cash-strapped public schools and channeled into private and/or more affluent public schools.

As is the case for standards and high-stakes testing, a close look at winners and losers of these initiatives demonstrates considerable benefit to corporate interests, once again at the expense of students and any dedicated teachers who still happen to be in classrooms despite the oppression of the high-stakes testing climate.

The Winners

Corporate interests. As noted above, publishing companies and other corporations have already derived significant economic benefits from passing though the doors of public schoolhouses. While those profits have been significant, they are barely the proverbial tip of the profitability iceberg.

> Education attracts the private sector for three reasons. First, it can be financially rewarding: Education is estimated to be a $600 billion market, more than the budget for the Department of Defense. The biggest single market is kindergarten through twelfth grade (K-12), valued at $310 billion in 1998. Additionally, lifelong learning and training programs for businesses and organizations are growing areas.
>
> Second, education has received such bad press that confidence in the established system is low, in spite of all the internal efforts at reform. . . . [H]ome schoolers and charter schools have increased, and both are customers for educational products and services. Home-schooling parents regularly attend regional conferences at which exhibitors offer their products and services. . . . Third, education is there for the taking: The general attitude is that professional, public educators have had sufficient time to turn the system around. (Buchen 1999)

The fact that the public has been consciously manipulated into believing that public school performance is much worse than it actually is has paved the way for corporations to increase their influence and to divide up this $600 billion pie in a number of ways.

An obvious area of profit that privatization brings for corporations involves the establishment of for-profit school management companies designed to make money for shareholders, companies that are widely seen as an entirely new area for investment and profit. Such firms are hired by cities to run their schools for them. While the idea of schools as money-making entities may be new to many readers, it's old news in the world of finance:

> The Wall Street term for private companies that wish to manage public schools is Educational Management Organizations (EMOs.) [sic] Proponents of privatization say that if you like HMOs, as many on Wall Street do, you'll love EMOs. The industry's backers are fond of comparing public education to the healthcare industry of 25 years ago, before the nationwide ascendancy of HMOs.
>
> "Education today, like healthcare 30 years ago, is a vast, highly localized industry ripe for change," Mary Tanner, managing director of Lehman Brothers, told a 1996 Education Industry Conference in New York City. "The emergence of HMOs and hospital management companies created enormous opportunities for the investors. We believe the same pattern will occur in education." (Miner 2002)

In these arrangements, the for-profit corporations typically assume all aspects of a school or district's operation with the clear intent of making a profit from the enterprise.

A typical representative of this trend is the Edison Project, run by Christopher Whittle—also the creator of Channel One. As 2002 opened, it was running 136 schools in 22 states and the District of Columbia; these arrangements placed education for some 75,000 children in its hands. Among those who have seen fit to invest in the "industry" and Edison are one of the co-founders of Microsoft, J.P. Morgan Chase & Co., and a Swedish holding company (Miner 2002). Clearly school management is very big business, and privatization offers enormous opportunity for various corporations to start making money on an enterprise that, theoretically, is intended to serve the best interests of children. However, as already discussed, the best interests of children and the best interests of corporations rarely coincide, since the needs of live children cost a great deal of money and the need of the managing corporation is to save on expenses in order to maximize profit. (The results of for-profit management to date will be discussed below.)

Once schools are managed by profit-making firms, it becomes easier and easier for companies producing various products to cooperate in deals that can produce revenue in a nearly limitless range of ways. In addition to providing curricular materials, tests, and school management, for example, corporations also stand to make money on an increasing reliance on other educational products, especially in the current high-stakes climate. These include "instructional" satellite programming like Channel One; a wide variety of software products from such companies as The Learning Company and Broderbund (which have merged); internet providers of curricular materials like *MarcoPolo;* tutoring by such companies as Kaplan and Sylvan; and, of course, an expanded range of computerized testing.

Some companies can—and more likely will—largely provide "one-stop" school shopping:

> With revenues of over $1 billion, Knowledge Universe is the most extensive educational competitor and supplier—a mega-brand. The brainchild of Larry Ellison, billionaire CEO of Oracle, and Michael Milken of junk-bond fame, the company aims to provide a lifetime of educational products and services. . . . Knowledge Universe already owns in whole or in part . . . Children's Discovery Centers of America, MindQ's Java Academy, Knowledge University, TEC Worldwide, and LeapFrog. These companies are estimated to be worth $4 billion–$6 billion. Knowledge Universe has also identified 31 additional industry segments for acquisition. One such candidate is Nobel Education Dynamics, which operates 100 preschools and over 30 private schools; Nobel [took] over its first charter school in 1999. (Miner 2003)

Education as an industry ripe for development seems to have permeated the consciousness of every segment of the corporate world.

More than one business writer waxes eloquent about endless profit possibilities in the wonderful future they foresee when schools are entirely in corporate hands:

> All indications are that public education will lose control of the field. Private competition, home schooling, and charter schools are draining off students, often good ones. Charter schools take away per capita dollars as well. Software programs are threatening to replace teachers. Testing will become a province of automated technology, often in partnership with textbook publishers and software developers. Finally, the lure of so much money will attract even more venture capitalists, who will aggressively carve up the future education market. (Buchen 1999)

There is no doubt that any step toward privatization is a windfall for corporate America.

The Losers

Students, and their teachers. Educational researchers have long known what steps will improve educational achievement, especially among disadvantaged students:

> [R]aising teachers' salaries, enhancing their training and professional development, instituting small classes in the early grades, creating high-quality preschools,

> providing tutoring and other individualized instruction where appropriate, improving the curriculum—substantial evidence shows that all of these changes do make a difference in outcomes for students, especially poor students. And all of them cost a lot of money. (Hochschild 2001)

Privatization, however, takes money *away* from children and schools by allowing corporations to run schools as profit-making enterprises.

And, despite great claims by companies like Edison that they can do a better job for less money than current public school administrators, there is no evidence to support the claim. In fact, experience to date indicates that at best, managed schools do as well as public schools—and often worse. Again, Edison provides a case in point.

> So far, say Edison's critics, it has not delivered the goods. "Edison has promised 'innovative curricula' that would revolutionize education," says Gerald Bracey, an education researcher. . . . "But, discovering that curricula cannot be developed easily, it had to fall back on existing curricula developed by orthodox educators. Edison students spend almost 50 percent more time in class each year than regular public school students and Edison emphasizes testing. Yet Edison students do not [perform] better than regular public education students. Edison vowed its schools could cost no more than regular public schools, but this promise, too, has been broken." . . . A recent study conducted for the National Education Association . . . found that Edison schools are performing the same as or slightly worse overall than comparable public schools. (Miner 2002)

There is no evidence that the money going into private pockets is in any way enhancing the education students receive. In fact, many charge that Edison "saves money by hiring less experienced teachers and that it does not adequately serve special education students" (Miner 2002).

Because education depends so heavily on the teaching force, it is a labor intensive industry; that is, much of the cost for running a school goes for teacher salaries. As the Edison experience demonstrates, one way for the for-profit management companies to save money is to hire less experienced teachers. Another way to save money—and for more companies to make more money—is to replace teachers entirely. This appears to be the direction corporations think schools should take.

As noted above, "teacher proof," scripted programs that are being promoted for classroom use already reduce the teacher to a robot-like classroom presence who simply implements programs designed by publishers. The kinds of phonics programs being promoted tell teachers what to say and when to say it; what activities to do and when and how to do them. This, however, may just be the beginning of how corporate influence may reshape the role of the teacher. Already, one tutoring company offers a tutoring program in which "teachers function as cheerleaders" (Buchen 1999). But in a for-profit school, more and more reliance on publishers' programs as well as on highly profitable electronic and other curricula and programs may make the teacher apparently *entirely* expendable:

> Almost all of the new educational products and services now being marketed bear the stamp of technology. Such technology replaces teachers altogether or reduces their number, thus solving several critical weaknesses in traditional education. For instance, replacing teachers reduces the high cost of an excessively labor-intensive instructional process while still serving the same number of students. Then, too, it eliminates tenure. . . . (Buchen 1999)

This completes the vicious cycle that teachers are currently caught in: they work in underfunded schools where "reforms" like high-stakes testing ensure that a large percentage of students will fail, they are denied professional development, they are forced into using programs from publishers—and then they are blamed for the failure while for-profit organizations plan to use the predetermined failure of students to eliminate teaching jobs. (In this context, that corporate interests have begun recruiting people from outside the field of education to train as "CEOs" of school districts seems ominous.)

Summary

Public schools are currently well along the road politicians and corporate leaders have been paving for some time: the public believes that its schools are failing; schools budgets have been gutted so that more and more schools must depend more and more upon partnerships with corporations for operating funds; high-stakes tests have been implemented that lead to more and more corporate profits and more and more student failure—especially for poor students; corporations have been increasing efforts to influence teacher and superintendent "training"; teachers have been increasingly losing classroom autonomy as they have been forced more and more into using profitable programs produced by publishers; vouchers have begun the process of channeling public money into for-profit hands, a significant step on the road to privatization; and, there is evidence that the job of "teaching" is increasingly being turned over to computers.

And, it is unlikely that these conditions will change simply with a change of faces in the White House. While much of this chapter is specific to the situation during George W. Bush's presidency, the trends described here are not unique to his administration. As noted in Chapter Four, NCLB is the product of a quarter century of political effort on behalf of corporations at the highest levels of American government.

With a change in presidents might come a change in which specific corporations benefit, but that corporations *will* continue to benefit seems unquestioned.

And yet: however much corporations—and Wall Street—may find the current conditions reasons to celebrate, many educators find them appalling and are devoted to a very different picture of the future of public schools and of the role of the teacher. This alternative vision is the subject of Chapter Six.

For Further Reading

Albrecht, S., & Joles, C. (2003). Accountability and access to opportunity: Mutually exclusive tenets under a high stakes testing mandate. *Preventing School Failure, 47*(2), 86–91.

Altwerger, B., Strauss, S. L., Labbo, L. D., & Bomer, R. (2002). The business behind testing. *Language Arts, 79*(3), 256–263.

Appleman, D., & Thompson, M. (2002). "Fighting the toxic status quo": Alfie Kohn on standardized tests and teacher education. *English Education, 34*(2), 95–103.

Buchen, I. (1999). Business sees profits in education: Challenging public schools. *The Futurist, 33*(5), 38–44.

Coles, G. (2003). *Reading the naked truth: Literacy, legislation, and lies.* Portsmouth, NH: Heinemann.

Coles, G. (2003, Summer). Learning to read and the 'W Principle', *Rethinking Schools Online* (Vol. 17). Available at http://www.rethinkingschools.org/.

Graves, D. (2002). *Testing is not teaching: What should count in education.* Portsmouth, NH: Heinemann.

Meyer, R. (Summer, 2003). Captives of the script: Killing us softly with phonics. *Rethinking Schools Online, 17*(4). Available at http://www.rethinkingschools.org/

Shepard, L. (2002/2003). The hazards of high-stakes testing [Electronic version]. *Issues in Science and Technology, 19*(2), 53–58.

Stevens, L. P. (April 2003). Reading first: A critical policy analysis. *The Reading Teacher, 56*(7), 662–669.

Welsh, P. (2003). Passing scores fail my students. *The Washington Post* (B 03). Washington, D.C.

CHAPTER 6

Critical Alternatives for Schools and Teachers

If you want democracy to be worth taking, you must be willing to pay a price.
It means doing the hard, often frustrating, deeply rewarding work of citizenship.
It means working with people we don't know, who get us out of our comfort zone,
with whom we disagree. . . . Democracy is the work of the people, of you and me.
If we stop doing the work, the value of the idea vanishes, politics becomes
narrow and nasty, and the door of tyranny opens.
CENTER FOR DEMOCRACY AND CITIZENSHIP

As the last two chapters have demonstrated, and as theorists have been claiming for decades, there is no such thing as a politically neutral curriculum; there is no such thing as a politically neutral school; and, there is no such thing as a politically neutral teacher. The question is not *whether* particular ideologies are being promoted, but *which* ones are—and how well we like them.

> Public education is inherently political in that public schools are places where citizens are made and particular visions of democracy are propagated. The questions that educators and other cultural workers need to ask are, "What kinds of citizens do we want to make?" and "What kind of democracy do we have?" (Saltman 2000, 117)

Current rhetoric and reform strategies embrace—as they always do—a vision that is wholly political and that privileges one group's definitions of "citizen" and "democracy" over others. Every educator must decide whether to endorse the prevailing vision or to work for change.

No matter how blandly every politician and citizen may endorse the notion that public schools are promoting democratic ideals, the current reality is that supporting *democracy* has come to be defined as supporting *that which best advances corporate goals for maximized profit.* Students have become little more than tomorrow's "human capital," and their education is being defined by businesses interested in maintaining not only a pool of highly skilled labor who will work for lower and lower wages, but also a pool of poorly educated workers who will accept the meanest work for minimal pay and also blame themselves for their failure to thrive in a land of "equal opportunity."

Moreover, students are being thoroughly indoctrinated with the message that ever greater consumption is the greatest social good. Rather than learning to define health, happiness, and success for themselves, children are learning that no matter how much they may have, they need more, with the result that:

> Studies already show that [teenagers'] favorite activity is shopping and that they spend on the average more than twenty dollars a day consuming . . . [They] see no value in hard work but . . . believe that value lies in status, and power lies in getting one's needs met, especially material needs. (hooks, 81)

As corporate mentality and influence have increasingly permeated the world of schooling, students—and with them American society at large—are increasingly at risk. Recently, Kenneth Saltman (2000) has written an impassioned warning about the threat of "mistaking corporate health for the well-being of the bulk of the population" (34), arguing that doing so constitutes a "threat to democracy." Already, there is plentiful evidence that the threat he warns against is being realized.

Casting citizenship as consumerism, and confusing corporate good with social good, for example, have already led to an unhealthy mania for goods and to a wide variety of social problems, excused by the privileging of corporate profit over all else. The picture of contemporary youth culture painted by bell hooks (2000) is a dismal one, though anyone familiar with that culture will recognize the portrait as true:

> Today's youth culture is centered around consumption. Whether it's wearing designer clothes or cruising in luxury cars, materialism becomes the basis of all transactions. For young people, the world is their marketplace. All one's worth, mass media advertising tells them, is determined by material things. Ironically, such thinking produces a symbolically "classless" society in that these values are shared by youth culture irrespective of race, gender, or class. . . . [Youth] are constantly told that the only peace and happiness they can have will come to them through rugged individualism, through a focus on meeting self-centered needs. . . . I find that the one common yearning children share, whether they are in fancy private schools with small classrooms or huge overcrowded institutions, is the longing to be wealthy. . . . already they are obsessed with getting. (81, 159)

The mania for getting, the assumption that money is the root not of all evil but of all good, focuses attention on individual wealth and distracts it from the health and happiness of the society at large. To buy things means having a job and a solid pay-check, which encourages the American public to accept corporate demands for a certain kind of worker. To the extent that educators and others accept job training as the primary goal of schools, schools will be pressured to conform to the corporate agenda that not only seeks to offer the lowest possible wages to all workers, but also to nurture students to become consumers driven by a lust for material goods.

In such a climate, an uncritical acceptance of any means to advance the ends of greater wealth and consumption has already wreaked social havoc in a wide variety of ways. As each citizen learns to look out for "number one," there is little sense of community, of connectedness to others, and little concern for how an act that brings some few individuals wealth in one place concurrently harms the well-being of countless others elsewhere. Overall, we suffer, even as many are unaware of the damage we have been imposing on ourselves during decades of corporate advance-ment, although critical theorists have been discussing it for some time in terms like these, from Giroux (1998):

> The power of corporate culture, when left to its own devices, respects few boundar-ies and even fewer basic social needs, such as the need for uncontaminated food, de-cent health care, and safe forms of transportation.

We lack uncontaminated food because of the chemicals needed to make corporate agriculture most profitable; we lack decent health care and safe transportation *only* for the many who can't afford to pay for the best health care the world has to offer or for luxury SUV's common among the wealthy few. David Solmitz (2001), too, protests the price we are paying for imposing a corporate agenda on all of society:

> It is imperative to reverse the trend that has brought about the fragmentation of so-ciety since the First Industrial Revolution. This disintegration has triggered compart-mentalization and standardization causing people to feel ever less connected with each other and with their natural environment. Our ecological environment has been devastated in the name of progress. Not only are our rivers and lakes polluted, our forests destroyed, our crops poisoned with herbicides, but many people live in large industrial cities where they live in fear and do not know their neighbors. A sense of community doesn't exist. An intimate connection with our biosphere has been dismantled. Therefore, as people become less sensitive and more imper-sonal toward one another, they easily become physically and emotionally abusive to-ward fellow human beings. Fewer people seem to feel a guilty conscience. Therefore, for example, laws have little impact upon them. Material wealth, instantaneous grat-ification, and reliance on the sensational for entertainment become the norm by which the majority of Americans seem to live. We take life for granted. (206–7)

Corporate scandal after corporate scandal has illustrated the truth in this character-ization of "anything goes" as long as it's in the interest of greater personal profit,

fostering cutthroat individualism and amoral profiteering along with a simultane-
ous loss of any concern for communal good and ethical behavior. What other kind
of citizen might we expect when schools advance uncritical consumerism and support for corporate agendas?

Solmitz (2001), among others, asks us to look hard at this kind of education and
to ask ourselves if the kinds of citizens that politicians and corporations are pressuring schools to produce match the kinds of citizens that educators and parents
themselves would hope to nurture:

- Do we want our children to grow up conditioned to the notion that success can
  only be measured in dollars and cents? Do we want to focus on values that articulate the elegance of the automobile we drive, the number of luxury items available
  to us, i.e., from big screen TVs to ATVs (all-terrain vehicles), from comfortable
  campers to Caribbean cruises?
- Do we want our children to continue to demand instant gratification: be it from
  sensational TV shows to credit cards that will soon be issued to them, to instant
  contentment provided by drugs and alcohol?
- Do we want our children to fight in wars in developing countries to preserve resources so that we can continue our rampantly materialistic lifestyle? Do we want
  to be held responsible for the innumerable deaths that may be caused by our military forces as well as the potentially enormous environmental damage created by
  such warfare? Do we want our children to become scientists, engineers, and man-
  ufacturers of the weapons that create ultimate devastation? (222–23)

To these questions, critical educators answer a resounding "No!"

In contrast, they make a strong case that rather than serving business, schools
should begin to serve humanity. They promote a much more encompassing vision of democracy, a much more humane understanding of the kinds of people—
of citizens—that schools should seek to nurture. In short, as an alternative to the
dehumanizing and socially devastating corporate agenda, critical educators propose very different visions of democracy, of educational goals, of schools, and of
teachers.

Critical Alternatives: Redefining Democracy and Democratic Goals

As early as 1914, John Dewey was writing and worrying about what he perceived as
government's natural tendency to create policy not for the masses of the governed—that is, not for the public at large—but for the relative few who wield
power in the existing social system. In relation to schools, he speculated about the
likely evolution of exactly the kind of situation described in the last two chapters,
in which politicians and a wealthy elite collaborate to produce educational policies
of benefit primarily to a select minority:

Is it possible for an educational system to be conducted by a national state and yet the full social ends of the educative process not be restricted, constrained, and corrupted? Internally, the question has to face the tendencies, due to present economic conditions, which split society into classes some of which are made merely tools for the higher culture of others. (97)

Dewey is one of many who have argued for safeguards against any state's tendency to use its schools to serve its own self-interested ends rather than to serve the good of its many citizens. This tendency means that even in a democracy, it is necessary to carefully monitor government to be sure that policies it promotes as being "in the best interest of the country" are not anti-democratic. Like Dewey, critical educators argue that if schools are to genuinely support the survival of a true democracy, then they must be places where the good of the many (all children and all citizens) takes precedence over the good of a few (privileged children, powerful politicians, and wealthy owners), and where a racially, linguistically, and culturally diverse population has equal access to quality education and opportunity for self-determination.

To these ends, Dewey argued that we must not only ensure that schools are "not actively used as an instrument to make easier the exploitation of one class by another," but we must also see that schools actively help offset the disadvantages some students experience at the start of their school careers. Schools must be sure that not only students of privilege, but also the many children living in poverty, the children who are not native English speakers—all children from divergent backgrounds—receive a quality education that allows them to become "masters of their own economic and social careers." Given what we know about the serious impact of such disadvantages, and given the intransigent funding inequities public schools continue to face, it may seem unrealistic to argue for a vision of schools that is serious about equipping every student with the skills and dispositions necessary to chart his or her own fate. However, as Dewey argued, it is a vision that schools in a genuinely democratic society must embrace:

The ideal may seem remote of execution, but the democratic ideal of education is a farcical yet tragic delusion except as the ideal more and more dominates our public system of education. (1914, 98)

In other words, to say that we are very far away from the goal does not excuse us from trying to attain it. To throw up our hands in despair is not to stay neutral, but to move ever farther away from the ideal. Surely any small step forward is preferable. Public schools must either move toward what they so often claim to be—the door to equal opportunity in American society—or remain a shameful, and potentially dangerous, deception perpetrated upon that society's least powerful members.

To move toward the vision of schools as places of genuinely equal opportunity, we must move away from the idea that "supporting democracy" means that schools must promote assimilation, that they must produce a standardized, and very specific type of citizen—specifically, a citizen happy to serve as "human capital" within a global economy, to consume voraciously, and to embrace the maxim "My country, right or wrong." In stark contrast, critical educators argue for schools that focus on people rather than things, on the many rather than the few, and on genuine rather than rhetorical democratic goals.

Arguing for what he calls "empowering education," for example, Ira Shor (1992) imagines schooling as "a critical-democratic pedagogy for self and social change." In this vision, schools are places where all students enjoy basic rights and learn to take an active role in shaping their own destinies by pursuing social change they believe desirable:

> Students in empowering classes should be expected to develop skills and knowledge as well as high expectations for themselves, their education, and their futures. They have a right to earn good wages doing meaningful work in a healthy society at peace with itself and the world. Their skills should be welcomed by democratic workplaces in an equitable economy where it becomes easier each year to make ends meet. To build this kind of society, empowering education invites students to become skilled workers and thinking citizens who are also change agents and social critics. (16)

As Giroux (1998) notes, such goals are *new* only in that they call for schools to renew their efforts toward "the democratic ideal of education" that Dewey stressed:

> One of the most important legacies of public education has been to provide students with the critical capacities, the knowledge, and the values to become active citizens striving to realize a vibrant democratic society. Within this tradition, Americans have defined schooling as a public good and a fundamental right (Dewey, 1916; Giroux, 1988). Such a definition rightfully asserts the primacy of democratic values over corporate culture and commercial values.
>
> Schools are an important indicator of the well-being of a democratic society. They remind us of the civic values that must be passed on to young people in order for them to think critically; to participate in policy decisions that affect their lives; and to transform the racial, social, and economic inequities that close down democratic social relations.

Similarly, Solmitz (2001) calls for schools to focus on "the self-actualization of each individual with an harmonious, socially responsible and happy integration into the local, state, national, and international community" (222), and Fischman (2000) argues for educators to embrace "the overarching purpose of contributing to increased social justice, equality, and improvement in the quality of life for all constituencies within the larger society." Giroux's terms for such democratic values and goals include "justice; freedom; equality; respect for children; and the rights of citizens as equal, free human beings" (1998).

Key to the vision of all such theorists is the need to encourage active, rather than passive, citizenship. It is ironic that this goal should constitute a major shift in direction, given the deeply ingrained, contemporary assumption that the foundation of democracy is a literate population that (theoretically) determines its own fate through the mechanism of elections. However, the vision of schools as institutions to nurture an active citizenry is in direct opposition to many entrenched educational methods.

> Dewey's connecting of participation with democracy underscored the political nature of all forms of education. Rote learning and skills drills in traditional classrooms do more than bore and miseducate students; they also inhibit their civic and emotional developments. Students learn to be passive or cynical in classes that transfer facts, skills, or values without meaningful connection to their needs, interests, or community cultures. To teach skills and information without relating them to society and to the students' contexts turns education into an authoritarian transfer of official words, a process that severely limits student development as democratic citizens. (Shor 1992, 18)

Precisely because traditional education focuses on the transfer of information and skills from anointed authorities with no regard whatever for the individual lives, circumstances and concerns of students, many young people find schooling—and any information about political life they may encounter there—irrelevant and so they often choose either to disengage from genuine intellectual engagement or to drop out of school altogether. This disengagement, prompted by the sterile rhetoric and routines of school authority figures, includes their withdrawal from any consideration of public life and active citizenship as well. Again, though decades old, Dewey's description of the outcomes of rote education are apt:

> Mass production is not confined to the factory. . . . [T]he endeavor to bring voters to a sense of their privileges and duties has so far been noted for failure. . . . Skepticism regarding the efficacy of voting is openly expressed, not only in the theories of intellectuals, but in the words of lowbrow masses: "What difference does it make whether I vote or not? Things go on just the same anyway. My vote never changed anything." Those somewhat more reflective add: "It is nothing but a fight between the ins and the outs. The only difference made by an election is as to who gets the jobs, draw the salaries and shake down the plum tree." (1927, 118)

Indeed, in 2002 the Bureau of Census reported that slightly fewer than half of all high school graduates registered to vote actually did vote in the 2000 presidential election, while for those who did not complete high school the percentage dropped to one-third to one-quarter of those registered.

And, despite mountains of research indicating the harm of imposing irrelevant and boring skill-and-drill pedagogies on students, the mania for testing, of course, has all but uniformly imposed such sterile methodology on schools at large, forcing teachers and schools to focus on test results at the expense of any pretense of modeling democratic habits of mind. As Shor (1992) notes, it doesn't matter if school authorities lecture students on freedom and democracy when the routines of classrooms prepare students "for the authoritarian work world and political system they will join" (19) by immersing them in a world of top-down authority, passivity, and self-interested competition:

> It certainly is not easy to create an atmosphere of mutual respect when the administration demands that students from kindergarten on are taught to follow the commands of the teacher and never to rely upon their own intelligence and insight. Nor is it easy to practice cooperation when the direction of the school is competition: striving for high grades, vying for athletic championships against other schools, running for class office or student council. Finally, since students have been conditioned to be passively obedient or face disciplinary consequences, it is often difficult for some to develop the self-discipline to listen to other students, to offer their own thoughts, and to realize that their input has been taken seriously. (212)

In direct contrast to such methodologies and classroom routines, the goal of education for active democratic citizenship calls for schools and classrooms that function very differently.

Critical Alternatives: Schooling for Participative Citizenship

The goal of a critical educator is to replace efforts to cultivate a blindly patriotic citizen with efforts to nurture an actively engaged one, a citizen who sees democracy not as an impersonal, irrelevant, and distant system but as a living and accessible one that offers them hope of changing their lives. Educating such a citizen means moving away from treating students as empty receptacles to be filled with received wisdom and toward encouraging them to become significant actors who play a key role in shaping the world/s they inhabit. To nurture such active citizens, Shor (1992) argues that schools must begin to abandon education as "a celebration of the existing society, as a falsely neutral avoidance of problems rooted in the system" and opt instead for "empowering" education, which he describes as "critical inquiry into power and knowledge as they relate to student experience" (13).

Education as Critical Inquiry for Social Change

The central element of critical reform, as implied in the term "critical inquiry," is the adoption of questioning as a central activity of the classroom. Students are encouraged to examine matters of importance to them, to ask why things are the way they are, to analyze who benefits most from the status quo, and to explore possibilities for changing conditions they don't like. Freire (1970) refers to such pedagogy as "problem-posing," and directly contrasts it with the "banking" pedagogy that casts students as passive receptacles for information:

> Whereas banking education anesthetizes and inhibits creative power, problem-posing education involves a constant unveiling of reality. The former attempts to maintain the *submersion* of consciousness; the latter strives for the *emergence* of consciousness and *critical intervention* in reality.
>
> Students, as they are increasingly posed with problems relating to themselves in the world and with the world, will feel increasingly challenged and obliged to respond to that challenge. Because they apprehend the challenge as interrelated to other problems within a total context, not as a theoretical question, the resulting comprehension tends to be increasingly critical and thus constantly less alienated. Their response to the challenge evokes new challenges, followed by new understandings; and gradually the students come to regard themselves as committed. (68–69)

The strategy is to ask students to examine aspects of their experience—of "the way things are"—that they have unconsciously accepted as inevitable facts of life. In this kind of education, teachers help students "develop their intellectual and emotional powers to examine their learning in school, their everyday experience, and the conditions in society" (Shor 1992, 12).

An obvious example of what it might mean to "examine their learning" appears in Chapter One of this text, in possible questions about what is and is not included in standard curricula—and why. Why memorize the date of the Bill of Rights without asking how constitutional rights relate to such issues as illegal searches and censorship of students in schools? (Such illegalities are common occurrences—see Hinchey 2001 and/or the American Civil Liberties Union website.) Why so much material about assorted wars and war heroes in history books and no mention of how Puerto Rico came under American control? Or how many treaties the federal government signed with Native American peoples and then violated? Or why the government paid to have "sportsmen" all but exterminate the buffalo? Even limited exploration in such areas makes immediately clear that no information or curriculum is politically neutral and allows students to think through their own conception of events and institutions.

Even more powerful, however, is the questioning of students' "everyday experience, and the conditions in society." Ladson-Billings recounts a story told by Tate (1994) about the power of engaging students in questioning their experience and environment and then, as Freire says is essential, allowing them to take action. The events took place

> in a city where zoning regulations meant that some areas of the city were wet (they allowed liquor sales) and other areas were dry. Not surprisingly, schools serving

low-income, African American, and Latino students were located in wet areas. After her students complained about constantly being hassled by the patrons of liquor stores and bars, the teacher got the students involved in a project that consisted of examining the zoning laws. The students took field trips and learned that schools in more resources-rich communities tended to be in dry areas. The students made observations in their own school community and documented the number of liquor stores in a short radius of their schools. Ultimately, the students worked on proposals for rezoning to present to the city council. (2001, 103)

Far from becoming the disengaged non-voters Dewey described and that largely populate contemporary American society, these students came to see themselves as having the right to ask about undesirable conditions in their immediate environment and then to take political action to provoke change. Surely such activity needs to be at the heart of education in service to democracy, to a political system that intends to allow the governed an effective voice in their communities and in society at large.

Of course, the results of such educational activity are likely to generate controversy. No doubt politicians and liquor store owners were happier before students started examining and trying to change zoning laws in their community. And, schools have historically not been places where anyone is expected to "make waves." In fact, as Solmitz (2001) points out,

education as a subversive activity that encourages students to look critically at their society, to raise questions, explore alternatives to transform it into a more beautiful, harmonious community is the antithesis of American education. (209)

Antithesis to tradition or not, however, no education that imposes a single, orthodox and unquestioned curriculum on students can be honestly labeled "democratic."

Although politicians are quick to call any opposition to their proposals and policies "unpatriotic" in order to cut off dissent, multiple perspectives on issues are, in point of fact, an inescapable and desirable element of a genuinely democratic society.

Democracy is a dynamic concept in which continuing social progress is an expectation and critical thinking is necessary. Education in a democracy is always in tension between the forces that resist change and those that press for change. Helping students sort out the elements, logic, and quality of evidence presented by these competing forces is the role of schooling in a democracy. (Daly, Schall, & Skeele 2002, 104)

The reasons for resistance to education as inquiry is, simply, that allowing voice for competing perspectives means that those currently in power are likely to encounter challenges to the world order they have imposed to serve their own interests. In fact, such challenges are precisely the ultimate goal of critical pedagogy, which intends to educate an active and critical citizenry equipped and inclined to pursue a more equitable distribution of advantage—a more just and equitable society and world.

Education in Service to the Many

Implied in the above discussion is a commitment to facilitating the entry of new voices into important public dialogues. In terms of the nature of schools, this commitment translates rather obviously into the recognition that diverse populations have diverse needs and interests, and it is the responsibility of schools to serve every population appropriately and well.

Among other casualties of standards and testing is the stark reality that children who come to schools from a wide variety of backgrounds cannot be pummeled into the same shape by nine or ten months in a classroom, no matter how many punitive policies are put into place for students, teachers, administrators and schools when children fail to be mass-produced on demand. Again, decades ago John Dewey (1914) was simply and eloquently demonstrating this obvious fact, which somehow seems to have escaped the notice of today's standards and testing enthusiasts:

> The educator, like the farmer, has certain things to do, certain resources with which to do, and certain obstacles with which to contend. The conditions with which the farmer deals, whether as obstacles or resources, have their own structure and operation independently of any purpose of his. Seeds sprout, rain falls, the sun shines, insects devour, blight comes, the seasons change. His aim is simply to utilize these various conditions; to make his activities and their energies work together, instead of against one another. It would be absurd if the farmer set up a purpose of farming, without any reference to these conditions of soil, climate, characteristic of plant growth, etc. . . . It is the same with the educator, whether parent or teacher. It is absurd for the latter to set up his "own" aims as the proper objects of the growth of the children as it would be for the farmer to set up an ideal of farming irrespective of conditions. . . . Any aim is of value so far as it assists observation, choice, and planning in carrying on activity from moment to moment and hour to hour; if it gets in the way of the individual's own common sense (as it will surely do if imposed from without or accepted on authority) it does harm. (106–7)

Schooling that fails to consider the differences among children is as likely to be as successful as the efforts of a farmer who plants corn despite the obvious fact his land constitutes a swamp.

Too often, schools ignore similarly crucial characteristics of children. How is the immigrant 9-year-old child who comes to school speaking no English to bene-fit from the same instruction as the American-born 9-year-old speaking fluent English—and to pass the same exams at the same time? How is the child who comes to school chronically hungry to care about the difference between *then* and *than*? Why do we expect the children who see adults able to secure only minimum-wage jobs—and unable to afford safe housing on their wages—to believe that a high school diploma will be their ticket out of poverty?

While the idea of standards and testing has superficial appeal in that it offers the *appearance* of equal opportunity, that appeal is deceptive because simply pretend-ing that life circumstances do not significantly affect school performance does not make it so. Comparable performance cannot be mandated or threatened into exis-tence; it must be nurtured with a wide array of support services that can genuinely narrow the learning gap created by living in poverty.

> Today teachers walk into urban classrooms with children who represent an incredible range of diversity. Not only are students of different races and ethnicities but there are students whose parents are incarcerated or drug-addicted, whose parents have never held a steady job, whose parents are themselves children (at least chronologi-cally), and who are bounced from one foster home to the next. And there are chil-dren who have no homes or parents. (Ladson-Billings 2001, 14)

As detailed in Chapter Three, there is extensive evidence that such factors place children at a distinct educational disadvantage, and such disadvantages take time, attention and extra resources to overcome. Instead of pretending that a one-size-fits-all system of threats can serve these children well, schools need to be structured to respond meaningfully to their needs, acknowledging that "all learning is some-thing which happens to an individual at a given time and place" (Dewey 1914, 108).

In addition to finding resources to help disadvantaged students overcome their formidable challenges, schools must also become places where *all* children are al-lowed to take pride in their unique cultural heritages while simultaneously adopt-ing an American identity. For too long, non-mainstream students have been treated as if they were deficient simply by virtue of being born with non-mainstream characteristics; education has aimed to erase their native identities in order to replace them with "superior" mainstream characteristics. Far from being democratic, such practices are perhaps the ultimate in intolerance and oppression. Children need not, and should not, be forced to accept the implication that the language and customs of their parents and homes is inferior. Attempts to force stu-dents to abandon one identity to assume the alien "American" identity schools pro-mote have long since proven sterile:

> In social conditions of unequal power relations between groups, classroom interac-tions are never neutral with respect to the messages communicated to students about

the value of their language, culture, intellect, and imagination. The groups that experience the most disproportionate school failure in North America and elsewhere have been on the receiving end of a pattern of devaluation of identity for generations, in both schools and society. Consequently, any serious attempt to reverse underachievement must challenge both the devaluation of identity that these students have historically experienced and the societal power structure that perpetuates this pattern.

Curriculum and instruction focused on empowerment, understood as the collaborative creation of power, start by acknowledging the cultural, linguistic, imaginative, and intellectual resources that children bring to school. (Cummins 2001)

To focus on what children cannot do rather than on what they can do is a disservice to them and their learning. Native American children, for example, are often taciturn—and erroneously judged as slow because of their apparent lack of verbal skill. Schools intent on understanding and valuing important cultural factors in students' home communities might instead choose to understand and value the sophisticated non-verbal language many Native American children employ—and in so doing, employ it in the service of improved student learning. Rather than trying to erase students' home languages and dialects as if they were inferior (an idea linguists have refuted for decades), schools need to begin thinking in terms of students developing multiple language forms.

And, if society itself is to become more just, not only school routines but student experience must be more inclusive. That is, students—all students—need to be exposed to greater cross-section of cultures than they may normally experience in the vast majority of public schools, which remain primarily segregated.

To become a community, students must learn to live in someone else's skin, understand the parallels of hurt, struggle, and joy across class and culture lines, and work for change. (Christensen 2000)

It is imperative that schools become places where information is examined from a wide variety of perspectives, and where the amount and kinds of information is not limited exclusively to that which advances an incomplete picture of the richness and diversity of America's history, people, and possibilities. Only through acknowledging and celebrating our diversity can the ideals of democracy be realized.

Critical Alternatives: Teachers Pursuing Social Justice

Obviously, a change in the goals and priorities in schools implies the need for a different kind of teacher. Teachers who embrace the vision of schools as sites where students are equipped to question their own circumstances and to pursue change where they think it warranted must develop different perspectives and habits, and they must acquire different kinds of knowledge than has been customary for public educators. For teachers who choose to follow the critical path, following is a survey of starting points for thinking through individual praxis. As with every facet of critical practice, there can be no one-size-fits-all formula for teachers to embrace. At a minimum, however, adopting a critical stance requires that the educator: engage in an honest and detailed examination of the way existing power structures shape experience, resulting both in unearned privilege for some and unfair disadvantages for others; offer students the respectful treatment, valid voice, and relevant curriculum that is their due as human beings; embrace the role of public intellectual, taking seriously the educator's opportunity and challenge to function as change agents in pursuit of a genuinely democratic society; and, accept the responsibility and need to engage in activism, no matter the discomforts and risks inherent in such work.

Teachers Who Understand Social Power Arrangements

Schools cannot become places where human growth and social justice are nurtured without the active engagement of teachers who understand what is at stake in classrooms. The forced imposition of standardized testing and of scripted pedagogical programs has been pushing the definition of "teacher education" in the direction of "teacher training." Such "training" involves preparing teachers to simply accept and implement the goals and agendas of corporate America, becoming robotic technicians who unquestioningly follow the instructions of others and who lack the temerity to ask how well those instructions serve their students. This training for mindless obedience equates to the same sort of training that forces circus animals to jump through hoops for the powerful and intimidating trainer.

Critical educators, however, hold a far different understanding of what constitutes education and what their roles in schools should be. The argument for "empowered" students applies equally to arguments for "Empowered teachers [who] understand the purposes of education and work to reform schools so they accomplish such purposes. Call it 'trickle-up reform'" (Kincheloe, Slattery, & Steinberg 2000, 251). To work for a particular agenda means, obviously, that teachers understand there is no way to avoid enacting *someone's* agenda, and that they consciously decide whether to support the status quo through unquestioning obedience or to pursue a different set of goals they personally find more desirable. That is, to oppose the corporate agenda, teachers must see clearly how deeply entrenched it is in current government policies.

A prerequisite for creating schools that more faithfully deliver on their democratic responsibilities is to educate teachers who understand education as a political activity and acknowledge the issues of power inevitably embedded in it:

> We use the term "political" . . . to address the concept of power, particularly the way power is distributed among definable social groups and types of individuals. All educational acts involve power. Who has access to school is a question that has been answered in many different ways throughout American educational history. African Americans, Latinos, migrant workers, immigrants, the poor, women—all have been denied access to schooling in general or to good schools or influential school programs in particular. We see here power-related issues, with some students gaining greater access to knowledge than others. (Kincheloe, Slattery, & Steinberg 2000, 276)

As long as the result of the current educational system is to ensure—despite the good intentions of countless individual educators—that students born to privilege retain privilege and students born without it remain without it, schools and teachers participate in a massive fraud perpetrated against America's schoolchildren. No movement toward social justice and genuine school reform is possible until educators grasp and act on this central understanding.

Many educators, notably those who work in the substandard schools so often provided for the poorest children, already have a deep understanding of the unfairness and inequities of the current system. One new teacher I know worked in a New York City school for only a few weeks before passionately protesting to me, "These kids are being set up for failure!" Many teachers are acutely aware that while their students, whose parents often struggle to keep food on the table, have to buy their own pencils and paper, children in affluent areas are provided with personal notebook computers at the school's expense. And, many teachers (and parents) of poor children are also fully aware that recently implemented standardized testing doom those children to academic, and subsequently economic, failure. The class of 28 children to whom this book is dedicated, for example, contains several students who speak not a single word of English—and yet, they will be expected to pass the same standardized exams within two years (perhaps sooner) as native English-speaking, middle-class children in far more affluent districts. Because the unfairness of such circumstances is blatantly obvious, grassroots organizations of teachers and parents lobbying for test boycotts are growing nationwide. Of course, teachers who work in the same kind of middle-class schools they attended themselves may be blissfully unaware of the very different conditions elsewhere, but those who work in poor schools are daily confronted, exasperated, and plunged into despair by the blatant inequity they and their students routinely suffer. *All* teachers need to understand that the privilege of one set of children comes at a price to others.

It is equally essential, if far more difficult, for *all* teachers to understand the impact of their own privilege, which can play out in the classroom in a variety of ways detrimental to students, intentionally or not. As Chapter Two detailed, the vast majority of teachers come from relatively privileged backgrounds, primarily White and middle-class. One of the most notable effects of such a background is that, since racial discrimination was unlikely to have been part of their life experience, they largely assume that racism is a thing of the past and that if poor children are in poor schools, it's because their parents lack the will to work that would have provided them with better educational opportunities.

Writing in 1997, Beverly Daniel Tatum outlines how little the White awareness of continuing, pervasive racism has grown:

> Early in my teaching career, a White student I knew asked me what I would be teaching the following semester. I mentioned that I would be teaching a course on racism. She replied, with some surprise in her voice, "Oh, is there still racism?" . . . Fifteen years later, after exhaustive media coverage of events such as the Rodney King beating, the Charles Stuart and Susan Smith cases, the O. J. Simpson trial, the appeal to racial prejudices in electoral politics, and the bitter debates about affirmative action and welfare reform, it seems hard to imagine that anyone would still be unaware of the reality of racism in our society. But in fact, in almost every audience I address, there is someone who will suggest that racism is a thing of the past. There is always someone who hasn't noticed the stereotypical images of people of color in the media, who hasn't observed the housing discrimination in their community, who hasn't read the newspaper articles about documented racial bias in lending practices among well-known banks, who isn't aware of the racial tracking pattern at the local school, who hasn't seen the reports of rising incidents of racially motivated hate crimes in America—in short, someone who hasn't been paying attention to issues of race. But if you are paying attention, the legacy of racism is not hard to see, and we are all affected by it. (3)

Tatum goes on to catalogue several ways "we are all affected," and the potential impact on teacher behavior in classrooms is easy to imagine.

For example, because most of us live in communities with others very like ourselves in race, religion and socioeconomic status, we have little firsthand knowledge of "the Other" (4–5). Lacking firsthand experience, we take our ideas from cultural stereotypes—which consistently cast non-mainstream people in terms of deficiencies. So it happens that teachers come to think of Native American children not as fluent in non-verbal language, but as inarticulate and slow; of African-American children not as active and creative, but as threatening and incorrigible. If non-White children don't complete their homework, it's not because of their own academic difficulties, but because their parents don't care about school and won't try to make them do it.

Many readers will deny that they make such stereotypical assumptions and instantly disclaim the possibility that any of their actions might embody unconscious racism. However, as Tatum (1997) details, the very fact of living in a segregated and racist society unavoidably influences our thinking and behavior—consciously or not.

> Prejudice is one of the inescapable consequences of living in a racist society. Cultural racism—the cultural images and messages that affirm the assumed superiority of Whites and the assumed inferiority of people of color—is like smog in the air. Sometimes it is so thick it is visible, other times it is less apparent, but always, day in and day out, we are breathing it in. None of us would introduce ourselves as "smog-breathers" (and most of us don't want to be described as prejudiced), but if we live in an environment in which we are bombarded with stereotypical images in the media, are frequently exposed to the ethnic jokes of friends and family members, and are rarely informed of the accomplishments of oppressed groups, we will develop the negative categorizations of those groups that form the basis of prejudice. . . . People of color as well as Whites develop these categorizations. (6)

Everyone absorbs cultural messages. Being exposed to countless pictures of Native Americans with feathers and tomahawks, we reproduce that picture mentally and assume that any contact with them means contact with an "uncivilized" culture; being exposed to countless pictures of large African-American males committing violence, we begin to fear such men, and we cross the street when an African-American man is approaching; or, as was the case when I began teaching high school, an African-American student who had encountered only racist teachers earlier in her experience took an antagonistic stance toward me on the first day of our year together in a predominantly White private high school, assuming I would not be genuinely interested in her education.

Even those of us most committed intellectually to equality may not yet have come to understand that intellectual commitment is not enough. Simply voicing opposition without taking action constitutes de facto support for the status quo. Critical educators understand the need to go farther, to embrace action as an essential component of practice.

> Prejudice is an integral part of our socialization, and it is not our fault. . . . To say that it is not our fault does not relieve us of responsibility, however. We may not have polluted the air, but we each need to take responsibility, along with others, for cleaning it up. Each of us needs to look at our own behavior. Am I perpetuating and reinforcing the negative messages so pervasive in our culture, or am I seeking to challenge them? If I have not been exposed to positive images of marginalized groups, am I seeking them out, expanding my own knowledge base for myself and my children? Am I acknowledging and examining my own prejudices, my own rigid categorizations of others, thereby minimizing the adverse impact they might have on my interactions with those I have categorized? Unless we engage in these and other conscious acts of reflection and reeducation, we easily repeat the process with our children. We teach what we were taught. (Tatum 1997, 6–7)

Tatum's questions are hard ones that all critical educators must ask of themselves—and answer honestly. For educators who accept the need to *act* on their answers, several imperatives become immediately obvious. Acknowledging and exploring the impact of their own backgrounds, as discussed in Chapter Two as well as in this section, is one. Others include developing genuine respect for and more authentic knowledge of "other people's children" as well as embracing the role that Giroux (1988) has named becoming "public intellectuals."

Teachers Who Respect the Other

While it is important to insist that "other people's children" deserve the same respectful treatment as children from the social and cultural mainstream, a prerequisite to that insistence is to insist that *all* children deserve more respect than they generally receive in the school environment. Teachers are expected to be "in control" of their classrooms and students, a situation that embodies autocratic rather than democratic norms. While classrooms cannot be chaotic, that doesn't mean—as is so often assumed—that the only alternative to chaos is a top-down "classroom management" system that offers students no rights and no voice.

In general, then, an immediate concern for critical educators is moving to pedagogical practice that creates classrooms that realize, rather than just vocalize, democratic principles. As Shor (1992) notes, every choice a teacher makes promotes one philosophy or another:

> Whether they deviate from or follow the official syllabus, teachers make numerous decisions—themes, texts, tests, seating arrangements, rules for speaking, grading systems, learning processes, and so on. Through these practical choices, the politics of the classroom are defined, as critical or uncritical, democratic or authoritarian. . . . Politics reside not only in subject matter but in the discourse of the classroom, in the way teachers and students speak to each other. The rules for talking are a key mechanism for empowering or disempowering students. How much open discussion is there in class? How much one-way "teacher talk"? . . . Do students feel free to disagree with the teacher? Do students respond to each other's remarks? Do they act like involved participants or like alienated observers in the exchange of comments in the classroom? Are students asked to think critically about the material and to see knowledge as a field of contending interpretations, or are they fed knowledge as an official consensus? Do students work cooperatively, or is the class a competitive exchange favoring the most assertive people? (13–14)

If the central pedagogy of schools is to become inquiry, then students must be free to suggest and explore issues of importance *to them;* if they are to learn to use their voices, they must first be allowed to develop and employ them in a safe and supportive educational environment, one where what they have to say is taken very seriously indeed; if they are to become citizens respectful of the rights and views of others, then they must be given practice listening to, understanding, and assessing a plurality of perspectives. Teacher and students should develop classroom rules jointly; all voices must share in respectful dialogue; shared responsibility, not tyranny, must characterize daily routines. In effect, critical educators promote a conception of the classroom as a community of learners, with the teacher being the most experienced learner—but still one learner among many, who respects and is willing to learn from students whose life experiences may be very different.

In fact, multiple perspectives must not only be encouraged and respected, but *ensured* as a critical element of the educational experience; students need a curriculum that "encourages them to empathize with others" (Christensen 2000). Of course, this equates to a call for multicultural education, and calls for a multicultural curriculum are hardly new. Unhappily, they too often have been dismissed as an attempt to impose "political correctness" at the insistence of self-interested, marginalized groups. The reality, however, is that a multicultural curriculum is essential if schools are to contribute to the creation of an authentically democratic society. Material from outside the traditional mainstream must be included in the curriculum not as appeasement to some groups, but as the only way to create a democratic community characterized by mutual understanding and respect. Few White teachers are familiar with other traditions, however, which is a distinct problem. As Howard (1999) proclaims in the title of his insightful book on the impact of Whiteness, "We can't teach what we don't know." It is an essential responsibility for every critical educator to assume responsibility for learning about other cultures and perspectives—most especially those in the home communities of their students.

As is true of teachers' efforts to recognize the impact of their own Whiteness (or other racial identity), efforts to acquire enough information about and understanding of other cultures to comfortably introduce classroom materials from them will be a difficult challenge for many educators. Still, it is an essential, and reachable, goal. Having extensive experience with mainstream representatives who support the goal of eliminating racism but feel paralyzed by their own lack of information, Tatum (1997) acknowledges the challenge even as she insists the goal is within reach:

> I have heard many people say, "But I don't know enough! I don't even recognize most of those names [of icons from a variety of cultures]. I don't have enough of the facts to be able to speak up about racism or anything else!" They are not alone. We have all been miseducated in this regard. . . . But we can learn the history we were not taught, we can watch the documentaries we never saw in school, and we can read about the lives of change agents, past and present. We can discover another way. (203–204)

Just as not being directly responsible for cultural racism doesn't absolve us from an obligation to work toward its elimination, not having been taught about other cultures does not absolve us from an obligation to learn about them.

The objectives of a multicultural curriculum don't need to be defended; they need instead to be understood as a core element of education for active democratic citizenship. Howard (1999) offers a useful summary of relevant objectives and the purpose they serve:

1. To know who we are racially and culturally
2. To learn about and value cultures different from our own
3. To view social reality through the lens of multiple perspectives
4. To understand the history and dynamics of dominance
5. To nurture in ourselves and our students a passion for justice and the skills for social action

When we structure our teaching and learning around these five basic components of multicultural education, we are contributing to the creation of a more just and open society.

It simply makes no sense to talk about democratic classrooms and respect for varied perspectives and then not include a wide variety of cultural voices in the curricular material that students spend so much time examining, reflecting on, and discussing.

Clearly, critical educators are people who believe that what they may have learned (or not learned) should not determine what they teach; who reject the idea that it makes sense for distant politicians and others to force a particular curriculum or assessment on students they have never met; who believe that their unique understanding of their specific students makes their voices essential in designing appropriate curricula and assessment. In short, the goals, attitudes and strategies detailed in this chapter call for a teacher who is very different from the compliant technicians corporations are trying to create and politicians are trying to bully into submission. Rather than puppets tied to the strings of commerce, teachers must become autonomous professionals, actively seeking substantive change.

Teachers as Public Intellectuals

For too long, teachers have been treated as hired hands and have been quietly following administrative instructions. As noted in Chapter Two, teaching's legacy as "women's work" has led to widespread disrespect for the difficult and demanding work good teachers attempt; the problem has been exacerbated by schools of education that, too often, have been more interested in an abundance of tuition dollars than in a rigorous education of the teaching force. I personally have worked with a great many teachers who simply accept powerlessness as a kind of occupational hazard. Teachers themselves, as well as the public writ large, need to begin challenging their diminished status and to insist on the active role that only they can execute as social change agents. As Saltman (2000) argues,

> Teachers need to recognize their role as public intellectuals. In this sense, teachers are not merely in the business of passing on knowledge but understand the significance of their practices as fostering particular social visions. By critically engaging students and curricula with regard to issues of power and politics, teachers, by virtue of their vocations, have tremendous power to counter "publicity intellectuals" in mass media who advocate oppressive and hierarchical social relations as well as unquestioned knowledge and authority. (118)

In order to pursue the goals of education in service to genuine democracy, teachers will first have to accept that they have an ethical responsibility to advocate on behalf of the welfare of students, which entails both a need to defend their own autonomy and to assume the role of activists and change agents themselves: "If a profession of teaching is to be realized, then teachers must realize that leadership comes with the territory" (Pellicer & Anderson 1995, 216).

Implementing a curriculum around inquiry and incorporating multicultural elements will not be possible until teachers insist that academic freedom be reinstated—that the trend to take control of the classroom away from them be reversed. Such pedagogical changes cannot be implemented—and "critical civic education" pursued—without "competent teachers who have the freedom to provide students with the freedom to examine controversial issues" (Daley et al. 2001, 105). Rather than passively allowing others to control their fate, teachers must begin to pay attention to the forces outside their classrooms that are working to control conditions within them, and they must begin to actively resist the imposition of distant, self-interested others:

> actions to denigrate, ignore, or destroy teacher participation in academic decision making deserve full attention from teachers and students, and opposition where needed. Such attention and opposition, however, require teachers to exercise academic freedom to challenge the government and local leaders, an effort that has not had much success so far. Meanwhile, the deskilling of teachers continues apace. (Saltman 2000, 119)

It is essential for teachers to recognize that the conditions they teach under have a direct impact on the future of their students, and that they are ethically bound to advocate for conditions that will, instead, offer their students more equitable opportunities.

Despite teachers' claims of powerlessness, tenure actually gives teachers the security they need to insist on sorely needed reforms. Unfortunately, however, tenure is not widely understood as the lever to accomplish change that it might be, either by teachers themselves or by the public at large:

> The primary role of teachers—to provide critical civic education for a democracy—is supported by tenure. Although the public usually understands why some job security is desirable, they seldom see why strong tenure laws are important, nor do they often see academic freedom as essential to education and democracy. Some members of the public believe that tenure allows incompetent teachers to keep their jobs and permits cunning teachers to brainwash their children. Too often teachers reflect this uninformed view that tenure is no more than a seniority-based employment benefit available to educators, not the basic protection for academic freedom as a right and responsibility of the profession. Some educators think that academic freedom and tenure are cosmetic excuses for doing whatever comes to mind. Such educators do not think academic freedom is worth fighting over if the administration or board of education wants to exert control, but these teachers will want the security of their tenure. This is an internal threat to academic freedom, because these teachers have no professional commitment to education in a democracy. (Daly et al. 2001, 108)

Teachers and anyone else holding the simplistic view of tenure simply as a form of job security must come to appreciate it—and defend it—as an essential tool in advocating for change on behalf of their students, no matter who opposes their efforts.

Nor is activism on behalf of academic freedom the only activism teachers must engage in. If they do not fight for a multicultural curriculum, who will? Or for schools that function as communities rather than as prison camps and/or factories? Or for adequate funding for children victimized by chronic inequities? All professionals bear ethical responsibilities to act always and everywhere on behalf of the best interests of their clients, and teachers cannot claim to be professionals without accepting the responsibility to advocate tirelessly for better teaching conditions and schools. Tatum (1997) acknowledges that that responsibility is a weighty one impossible to embrace with a light heart, but also catalogues a wide variety of ways anyone can begin to take an activist stance:

> Do you feel overwhelmed by the task? . . . Sometimes I feel overwhelmed, too. The antidote I have found is to focus on my own sphere of influence. I can't fix everything, but some things are within my control. While many people experience themselves as powerless, everyone has some sphere of influence in which they can work for change, even if it is just in their own personal network of family and friends. Ask yourself, "Whose lives do I affect and how? What power and authority do I wield in the world? What meetings do I attend? Who do I talk to in the course of a day?" (204)

Where any individual teacher may begin to pursue change is far less important than *that* they begin to pursue it. No step is too small to be worth taking if it leads forward toward a more just world.

Of course, authorities can resist change much more readily when they can dismiss calls for it as coming from lone cranks, perpetual malcontents who just don't know how to go along to get along. But we know that a critical mass of people speaking with a single voice—as they did during the Civil Rights movement that changed American society forever—makes an enormous difference in determining whether or not a message gets attention. It follows, then, that part of any educator's activism must include finding and uniting with like-minded others. As Saltman (2000) urges, "Teachers need to connect their struggles and practices to the vibrant and prolific array of contemporary social movements" (119). There is no shortage of allies: the labor movement; grassroots community groups, including parents banding together to resist the recently mandated standardized testing; multiculturalists; environmentalists, and many others. Because it is crucial that educators become involved in such movements, helping to magnify the volume of messages to politicians and others, the appendix following this chapter offers a sampling of the kinds of groups that exist and are already working toward the more just society critical educators envision. Rather than an exhaustive list, it is simply a preliminary road sign to the limitless resources and allies that lie a few clicks away from critical educators in cyberspace.

Teachers as Risk-Takers

I have long felt that teacher educators do students no favors by calling for such action without being candid about the risks involved, especially to teachers who are not yet tenured. Elsewhere (Hinchey 1998) I have told the story of how I happened to lose my first teaching job by defending a "scholarship boy" when the elitist private school we inhabited decided to make an example of him for drinking—after administrators chose not to make an example of others they had caught, whose parents were generous contributors to the school. In my own classes, I often tell my students that I'm fairly convinced that a willingness to be fired for actively protesting unjust treatment of students is a prerequisite for being a "good" teacher. Many think these ideas odd, or discouraging, but I would argue that it does no good to send teachers into a fray without warning them ahead of time about the landmines likely to lay ahead. Forewarned is forearmed, and given the ferocity of those who already wield most power, the least we can do is to warn new activists of the need to prepare for future fireworks.

My own story is only one of many about the dire consequences that can befall teachers who challenge the powers that be. For example, a Colorado school district found it inappropriate for a tenured high school teacher to show a particular film about fascism (Bertolucci's *1900*). Despite some ten years' work as an exemplary educator in Colorado and earlier successful teaching experience in Vermont, the teacher was dismissed for using unapproved materials in the classroom. Fortunately, the Colorado Education Association as well as the American Association of University Professors (AAUP) helped the teacher take the issue to a hearing, which he won. His principal, however, continued to try to fire him on such petty pretenses as being late to faculty meetings. While the teacher eventually won challenges to the principal's actions, the experience was a long and arduous one, consuming much of the teacher's energy and time and very likely providing significant discouragement to other teachers who might be interested in acting on the academic freedom that theoretically exists in their classrooms (Daley et al. 2001, 105). While the dangers of harassment and such punitive actions are real for teachers who challenge the status quo, equally real is the support of allies like unions and other professional associations, as well as watchdog organizations like the American Civil Liberties Union (ACLU) and People for the American Way. Yes, exercising academic freedom and taking political action can result in personal turmoil. But to say that activism can result in personal difficulty is not to offer a legitimate excuse for evading the educator's responsibility to advocate for policies in students' best interests. Rather, instead of avoiding possible controversy, critical educators must take seriously the need to network with likeminded others who can provide substantive support should a crisis evolve. Those who avoid activism because of possible personal danger keep themselves safe—but they fail to fulfill their ethical responsibility to be active advocates for the children entrusted to their professional care.

Parting Thoughts

This book is dedicated to a room full of real children and one new teacher who are living the issues outlined in these chapters. The dedication is intended to serve two purposes: to signal to children and teachers currently suffering under current conditions that there are others aware of their plight and working to help change those conditions; and, to remind readers that the theoretical issues explored here ultimately have a human face and real consequences for living, breathing children. The need for the kind of awareness and advocacy described here is urgent:

> many poor and minority students find that the world they have been told to trust no longer works. As they see their impoverished childhoods ending, these students assume adult responsibilities with headlong speed. Looking back they realize that someone has stolen their dreams and replaced them with narrow choices and a diminished sense of self. Youth suicide was hardly even a statistic before 1960; by the

1980s it had become second only to accidents as the leading cause of death among young people. By the 1990s youth suicide was being described as an epidemic. By the time many children enter high school vocational education they are already world weary and drained of any hopeful expectation. They have "heard it all": the phonies peddling their manipulative pseudohope based on everything from televangelism to drugs to schooling. They have acquiesced in the false prophets of education-for-success who shunt them into the low-track classes, and they have figured out the consequences of this deceitful process (Ferguson, 1994; Gaines, 1990; West, 1993). (Kincheloe, Slattery, & Steinberg 2000, 342)

The stakes are high, the needs of children great.

It is my earnest hope that these pages have persuaded readers to care about America's "other" children—to accept the role of public intellectual and the goal of social justice and to begin actively pursuing political power and real educational and societal change. As Perreault (2000) notes,

> It will be crucial to develop pockets of resistance within the system itself. This will be difficult and sometimes even dangerous work because, as Cohen [has said], "To expect that a state will allow its schools to serve aims other than those of the national policy is to expect that a state will not act like a state."

Despite the difficulty and the danger, educators must begin resisting the status quo and displaying resistance. It is my hope that the following appendix, which points to ready sources of information and a wide variety of allies, makes it easy for readers to take the next step on the challenging path to becoming a critical educator.

For Further Reading

Daly, J. K., Schall, P. L., & Skeele, R. W. (Eds.). (2001). *Protecting the right to teach and learn: Power, politics and public schools.* New York: Teachers College Press.

Howard, G. R. (1999). *We can't teach what we don't know: White teachers, multiracial schools.* New York: Teachers College Press.

Keresty, B., O'Leary, S., & Wortley, D. (1998). *You can make a difference: A teacher's guide to political action.* Portsmouth, NH: Heinemann.

Kincheloe, J. L., Slattery, P., & Steinberg, S. R. (2000). Chapter 8: Empowering teachers. *Contextualizing teaching.* New York: Addison Wesley Longman.

Ladson-Billings, G. (2001). *Crossing over to Canaan: The journey of new teachers in diverse classrooms.* San Francisco: Jossey-Bass.

Perry, T., & Delpit, L. (1998). *The real ebonics debate: Power, language and the education of African-American children.* Boston: Beacon Press.

Purpel, D. (2001). *Moral outrage in education.* New York: Peter Lang.

Seltzer, R., Frazier, M., & Ricks, I. (1995). Multiculturalism, race and education. *Journal of Negro Education, 64*(2), 124–140.

Solmitz, D. (2001). *Schooling for humanity: When big brother isn't watching.* New York: Peter Lang.

Stratman, D. (1997). *School reform and the attack on public education* . Keynote Address to the Massachusetts Association of School Superintendents Summer Institute. Available at http://www.newdemocracyworld.org/edspeech.htm.

Tatum, B. D. (1997). *"Why are all the Black kids sitting together in the cafeteria?"* New York: Basic Books.

Wink, J. (2000). *Critical pedagogy: Notes from the real world* (2nd ed.). New York: Longman.

Information and Allies
for the Critical Educator

Applied Research Center
3781 Broadway
Oakland, CA 94611
(510) 653-3415
www.arc.org
e-mail: arc@arc.org
Established in 1981, ARC describes itself as "a leading research lab and foundry where academics and activists forge tools to spark social progress and measure the results."

Its research focuses on issues related to race, media, activism and culture; it looks closely at public policy, education, research, and most especially, practice and issues surrounding organizing. It published the landmark report *Beyond the Politics of Place,* a study of community organizing around issues of identity of the marginalized: people of color, gays and lesbians, and women. ARC details its work in two publications: *RaceFile* (a leading reference journal) and *ColorLines* (a magazine).

Center for Community Change
1000 Wisconsin Avenue, NW
Washington, DC 20007
(202) 342-0519
www.communitychange.org
e-mail: info@communitychange.org
The essence of the work done by the center for Community Change is grassroots community building through self-help, development of leaders, critical services,

business development, home building, and community activism. Through these initiatives, the Center hopes for reductions in poverty and the rebuilding of low income communities. Ultimately, its goal is to assist low-income communities, especially those whose populations are people of color, to "build powerful, effective organizations through which they can change their communities and public policies for the better."

Center for Economic Conversion
222. View Street
Mountain View, CA 94041
(650) 968-1126
www.conversion.org
e-mail: cec@igc.org
Founded over 23 years ago, this non-profit educational and research group is committed to building an economy that not only meets social needs, but an economy that also is compatible with environmental and ecological concerns. One current project of the CEC is the effective redevelopment of closed or to-be-closed military installations. Organizational goals include sustainable economic development, public education about reinventing the economy, and promoting public policies for equitable and sustainable local, regional, and national economic development. Additional programs include green conversion activities, targeted educational outreach, and public policy shaping.

Children's Defense Fund
25. E Street, NW Washington, CD 20001
www.childrensdefense.org
e-mail: cdfinfo@childrensdefense.org
The familiar slogan "leave no child behind" emerged from the Children's Defense Fund. The group wants to guarantee each and every child a good start (a Healthy Start, a Head Start, a Fair Start, a Safe Start and a Moral Start) through the help of family and community. Founded to provide a forum for all children who are without a voice, the group specifically provides extra support to poor, minority, and disabled children.

Coalition of Essential Schools
CES National
1814 Franklin Street, Suite 700
Oakland, CA 94612
(510) 433-1451
www.essentialschools.org
e-mail: ksimon@essentialschools.org or vcoleman@essentialschools.org

This reform program founded by Ted Sizer (a leading U.S. educational reformer) asks communities to examine their priorities in terms of creating small, vibrant, personalized schools that are intellectually challenging. The guiding principles for CES schools call for personalized instruction, small learning communities with high expectations, multiple forms of assessment, equitable and democratic policies/practice, and strong links to the community. The web site contains publications, projects, membership information, forums, and resources.

CorpWatch
2288 Fulton Street, #103
Berkeley, CA 94704
(510) 849-2423
www.corpwatch.org
e-mail: corpwatch@corpwatch.org
The slogan of this San Francisco Bay Area–based organization is "holding corporations accountable." The group is at the leading edge of the movement protesting and acting against corporate-led globalization. Sucessful CorpWatch initiatives include radio broadcasts from the Seattle WTO protests, and pressuring Nike to improve sweatshop conditions. The organization's web site is robust and includes action alerts, issues, research and research tools, publications, a library, an e-mail newsletter, and information on campaigns.

Digital Freedom Network (DFN)
520. Broad Street, 3rd Floor
Newark, NJ 07102
(973) 438-1735
www.dfn.org
e-mail: DFNinfo@dfn.org
The Digital Freedom Network (DFN) promotes freedom through education about politics, economics, and current events via the Internet. Based on networking among those interested in upholding freedom, DFN highlights issues and current events, provides articles and essays, offers a forum for people without freedom of speech in their country, and makes technical information available to freedom activists. The group fights against any degradation of individual liberties in favor of state control.

Dollars & Sense
740. Cambridge Street
Cambridge, MA 02141
(617) 876-2434
www.dollarsandsense.org

e-mail: dollars@dollarsandsense.org

Dollars & Sense describes itself as a magazine for economic justice, offering alternative perspectives on the economy and economic affairs. Published since 1974, the magazine is bimonthly. The web site offers a selection of pieces from the current issue as well as archives. The organization also publishes books and article anthologies targeted for classroom use.

Economic Policy Institute

1660 L Street N.W. Suite 1200

Washington, D.C. 20036

(202) 775-8810

epinet.org

e-mail: epi@epinet.org

The Economic Policy Institute (EPI) is a corporation funded mostly by foundation grants, but also by individuals, corporations, government agencies and labor unions. The group is research-oriented and focuses on living standards/labor markets, government and the economy, globalization and trade, education, and retirement policy making. Fundamentally, EPI wants to develop the public debate about how to achieve a fair and prosperous economy. One feature included on EPI's web site is JobWatch (at www.jobwatch.org) which tracks wages and job growth, measuring them against the Bush Administration's projected number of jobs created by the 2003 tax cut.

Environmental Working Group (EWG)

1436 U Street, NW, Suite 100

Washington, DC 20009

(202) 667-6982

www.ewg.org

e-mail: info@ewg.org

Funded primarily by foundation grants, this research and public interest watchdog organization is committed to improving public health and reducing air, water, and food pollution. The research prepared under the auspices of EWG is transformed from raw data to useful information through reports and publications. The EWG web site contains information about current facts and figures, and archives of all reports.

The National Center for Fair & Open Testing (FairTest)

310. Broadway

Cambridge, MA 02139

(617) 864-4810

www.fairtest.org

email: info@fairtest.org

This center's goal is to end misuse, flaws, and abuses present in standardized testing. The staff and supporters of FairTest are committed to ensuring that evaluation of students and workers is "fair, open and educationally sound." In particular, the organization seeks to expose and eliminate test bias due to class, race, gender, and other cultural factors. The web site describes the details of various projects such as assessment reform, new assessment frameworks, employment testing, and questioning financial aid eligibility based on SAT/ACT scores.

Gay, Lesbian and Straight Education Network (GLSEN)

121 West 27th Street, Suite 804

New York, New York 10001

(212) 727-0135

www.glsen.org

e-mail: glsen@glsen.org

The GLSEN network is devoted to creating safe school environments for lesbian, gay, bisexual, and transgender students as well as other members of the school community. Its goal is to create schools in which all people are respected regardless of gender identity/expression and sexual orientation. The network's objectives involve organizing at a local level, shaping public opinion and policy, helping students understand and fight for their rights, and teacher education.

Global Exchange

2017 Mission Street, #303

San Francisco, CA 94110

(415) 255-7296

www.globalexchange.org

e-mail: admin@globalexchange.org

Founded in 1988, Global Exchange is devoted to promoting justice in the areas of society, politics, and the environment. A further goal is to help enhance global awareness within the United States while simultaneously building worldwide partnerships. Activities of Global Exchange include linking people to people, managing fair trade stores, publishing resources on human and economic rights, and sponsoring "reality tours" to developing countries.

In These Times

2040 North Milwaukee Avenue

Chicago, IL 60647

(773) 772-0100

www.inthesetimes.com

e-mail: sarver@inthesetimes.com

Published biweekly for nearly 40 years, *In These Times* is a national magazine of opinion and news. It has provided cultural criticism about news, events, and ideas as well as stories on labor, ecology, the women's movement, media, and corporate/governmental irresponsibility. The web site features articles from the archives, weblogs, material from the current issue, and news.

Independent Media Center
1415 Third Avenue
Seattle, WA 98101
Attn: Indymedia Network.
www.indymedia.org
e-mail: help[@t]indymedia.org
Organized primarily via the Internet and e-mail lists, the Independent Media Center (Indymedia or IMC) is "a collective of independent media organizations and hundreds of activists/journalists offering grassroots, non-corporate coverage." There are over 50 autonomous IMCs and web sites in the world today providing local visions and coverage, in addition to the international web site listed above. The goal of both the umbrella network and the local groups is to provide "open publishing" forums via a variety of media for independent reporting of political and social issues. Unless specifically noted by the author, all original content on Indymedia is free for reprint and rebroadcast.

International Forum on Globalization
1009 General Kennedy Avenue #2
San Francisco, CA 94129
(415) 561-7650
www.ifg.org
e-mail: ifg@ifg.org
Believing that institutions such as the World Trade Organization (WTO) and the Free Trade Area of the Americas (FTAA) combine to create and maintain a global system of privatization, liberalization, and deregulation without public disclosure as to consequences, the IFG seeks to respond. The International Forum on Globalization began as an activist think tank, envisioning ways to counter global governance by transnational corporations and to help reverse the globalization process through local economic and ecological initiatives. Today it involves over 60 scholars, researchers, and economists representing over 60 organizations in 25 countries who are allied in response to economic globalization.

Jubilee USA Network
222. E. Capitol Street, NE
Washington, DC 20003

(202) 783-3566
www.jubileeusa.org
e-mail: coord@j2000usa.org
In support of canceling the debt burden of developing countries, the Jubilee network encompasses churches, labor, AIDS activists, and social activists. Claiming that international debt is a form of slavery with workers continuing to toil in order to pay interest on loans from rich countries and global financial institutions, Jubilee's goal is to provide advocacy strategies for workers in addition to educational outreach efforts.

Labor Notes
7435 Michigan Ave
Detroit, MI 48210
(313) 842-6262
www.labornotes.org
e-mail: labornotes@labornotes.org
Since 1979, Labor Notes has been active in regaining the power of the labor movement lost in recent decades. Its non-profit activities include *Labor Notes* magazine (some articles are available online), print materials, conferences, and schools/training for labor union activists. The Internet site lists current labor news, conference information, articles from the current issue of the magazine, a bookshelf, and a selection of music associated with the labor movement.

MoveOn
www.moveon.org
e-mail: info@moveon.org
The fundamental idea behind MoveOn is to engage ordinary people in politics by building electronic advocacy groups. Advocacy groups are built when there is a gap between legislative and policy-making activities and broad public opinion. The group is funded by grants, individual citizen's contributions, and donations from its online membership of over 2 million people. MoveOn ensures the voices of its membership are heard by soliciting issues, priorities, and strategies and asking members to decide on what direction the organization should take.

Moving Ideas Network
2000 L Street NW, Suite 717
Washington DC, 20036
(202) 776-0730
www.movingideas.org
e-mail: movingideas@movingideas.org
Formerly the Electronic Policy Network, Moving Ideas Network (MIN) is an

Internet source for learning about progressive public policy. MIN filters through and posts ideas and resources from progressive institutions and also provides current research reports. The web site hosts a number of features including: resources and research from member organizations, essential facts about legislative issues, current policy-making efforts, short articles and statistical data, a weekly website highlight, "hot" issues of the day, and other resources such as jobs and community events.

National Coalition of Education Activists

1420 Walnut Street, Suite 720
Philadelphia, PA 19102
(215) 735-2418
www.nceaonline.org
e-mail: ncea@aol.com
The National Coalition of Education Activists (NCEA) believes in excellent and equitable schools, pursuing this belief by assisting students in reaching their potential and supporting efforts toward building an equitable society. Made up of a multiracial membership that includes school teachers, staff, parents, union members, child advocates, and community activists, NCEA offers ways for multiracial groups to talk about educational issues and solutions; develops knowledge and skills for activists; creates and publishes materials (see web site: Action for Better Schools); and disseminates information and referrals on activism (see web site: Resources for Better Schools).

The National Labor Committee

540. West 48th Street, 3rd Floor
New York, NY 10036
(212) 242-3002
www.nlcnet.org
e-mail: nlc@nlcnet.org
Established in 1995, the National Labor Committee, in support of human and worker rights, uses publications, media events, educational opportunities, social activism, and research to promote living wages and dignified lives for workers worldwide. Partnering with NGOs, unions, and individual workers, the NLC exposes abuses and publicizes examples of the "race to the bottom"—a consequence of the global economy that causes workers to compete against each other for the lowest wages and benefits.

NetAction

P.O. Box 6739
Santa Barbara, CA 93160
(415) 215-9392

www.netaction.org
e-mail: info@netaction.org
Dedicated to using the Internet for grassroots citizen action campaigns, and educating policy makers, media, and the general public about technology policy concerns, NetAction is a project of the non-profit Tides Center. NetAction is devoted to ensuring technological accessibility and affordability, training activists to use the Internet as an outreach, advocacy, and organizing tool, and linking cyberspace activists with grassroots organizations. This site offers a training course called *The Virtual Activist.*

New Democracy

P.O. Box 427
Boston, MA 02130
(617) 323-7213
www.newdemocracyworld.org
e-mail: Newdem@aol.com
New Democracy works toward the overthrow of dictatorship by the wealthy, not through Marxism, socialism, or communism, but through the struggle of ordinary people to humanize the world. Links on the web site include a newsletter, a statement of principles, relevant links to other resources, and collections of pages based on "worlds" of education, war, health care, revolution, and work.

New Internationalist

PO Box 1062
Niagara Falls, NY 14304
(905) 946-0407
www.newint.org
e-mail: magazines@indas.on.ca
The publications and web presence of New Internationalist report on concerns about inequality and world poverty. With a goal of focusing attention on the unequal dynamics between those in power and those who are powerless, the magazine brings the perspective of the latter to the fore. The company, independent of religious and political organizations, produces a variety of vehicles (magazine, educational materials, film, etc.) to communicate its message of worldwide social justice.

Organizers' Collaborative

Box 400897
Cambridge, MA 02140
www.organizenow.net
e-mail: oc@organizenow.net
An educational and charitable non-profit, Organizers' Collaborative seeks to assist

those working for social change via furthering potential computing technologies to increase communication and collaboration. The group organizes and disseminates information about grassroots uses of technology, develops software applicable to social change initiatives, provides online means of collaborating and sharing of resources, and offers some limited technical assistance to grassroots movements. The collaborative offers a national directory of social change e-mail lists and forums, organized by constituency, geographic area, region, and issue via the web site www.democracygroups.org.

Pencils Down

Pencilsdown.org
e-mail: Linda@pencilsdown.org or gray@pencilsdown.org
Described as a grassroots web-based gathering place for those concerned with "mis-education of children in the name of standardized test scores," PencilsDown provides news, strategies and tactics, information, arguments for authentic assessment, and ways to support educators opposed to standardized testing initiatives. Using the slogan "there's nothing standard about children," this site makes available links to articles, books, and other like-minded organizations.

People for the American Way

2000 M Street NW, Suite 400
Washington, DC 20036
(202) 467-4999 or (800) 326-7329
www.pfaw.org
e-mail: pfaw@pfaw.org
PFAW, or People for the American Way, aims to maintain as well as advance the cause of social justice by fighting against the right-wing agenda. Believing in the values of diversity and democracy, PFAW, along with progressive national and state agencies, works toward mobilizing the American public to stand up against the pressure of the radical right. Some of the causes on PFAW's agenda are threats to the Constitution, establishing an independent judiciary, ensuring public education, and advancing the current state of civil and equal rights.

Political Research Associates

1310 Broadway, Suite 201
Somerville, MA 02144
(617) 666-5300
www.publiceye.org
email: pra@igc.org
Political Research Associates (PRA) and their web pages located at "The Public Eye" promote a progressive agenda and work to advance a democratic, open, and

pluralistic society. The organization is a non-profit independent research institution studying oppressive, antidemocratic, and authoritarian movements. The Internet site provides links to like-minded resources, information, materials, and references. PRA publishes a periodical three times a year, also called *The Public Eye,* and offers special reports, activist resource kits, and speakers for workshops and conferences.

Positive Futures Network
P.O. Box 10818
Bainbridge Island, WA 98110
(206) 842-0216 or (800) 937-4451
www.yesmagazine.com
e-mail: yes@futurenet.org
Publishers of the magazine *Yes! A Journal of Positive Futures,* Positive Futures Network (PFN) is a nonprofit agency that encourages active participation of citizens in creating equity and sustainability at all levels of society. The agency asserts that its networking and communications initiatives have been successful at overcoming cynicism about the state of contemporary society. The web site contains discussion guides for the magazine which are targeted toward helping young people understand the breadth and depth of the world's social and ecological problems. The site also publishes lists of resources and relevant events, and identifies conferences and information sharing opportunities.

Resource Center of the Americas
3019 Minnehaha Avenue
Minneapolis, MN 55406
(612) 276-0788
www.americas.org
e-mail: info@americas.org
Resource Center of the Americas is a non-profit organization committed to fundamental human rights. The work of this action-oriented group involves teaching and learning about the people and countries of the Americas through the lens of global economy. Americas.org is a program emerging from the Resource Center of the Americas that offers alternative sources of information, action alerts, voices from developing countries, media analysis, events listings, books, publications, workshops and opportunities for youth organizers.

Rethinking Schools
1001 E. Keefe Avenue
Milwaukee, WI 53212
(414) 964-9646 or (800) 669-4192

www.rethinkingschools.org
e-mail: webrs@execpc.com
Emerging from Milwaukee-area school teachers in 1986, this non-profit publisher of educational materials is directed by volunteer editors and editorial associates assisted by a small staff. Rethinking Schools is committed to the idea that developing a humane, equitable, and multiracial democracy is centered in public education. Activist-oriented teachers, parents, and students write publications and articles often oriented toward urban educational issues. The web site contains a variety of articles, links to resources, archives, and publications.

Susan Ohanian

www.susanohanian.org
e-mail: SOhan70241@aol.com
Susan Ohanian (free-lance author, teacher, anti-testing activist) maintains a web site that presents information on educational issues through commentary, letters, cartoons, and links to resources. Regular features also include sections on Atrocities, Outrages of the Day, and Research That Counts.

Sweatshop Watch

310. Eighth Street, Suite 303
Oakland, CA 94607
(510) 834-8990
www.sweatshopwatch.org
e-mail: sweatinfo@sweatshopwatch.org
Founded in the early 1990s, this group is a federation of labor, civil and immigrant rights, women's, student, and religious organizations, as well as individual people concerned about exploitation of workers. With over 30 member organizations, two major projects of Sweatshop Watch are a corporate accountability campaign and a project intended to assist garment workers impacted by an increasingly globalized economy. Although California garment workers have been its target population, the coalition serves all low wage workers by insisting on living wages and holding employers accountable for abusive conditions.

Teaching for Change

P.O. Box 73038
Washington, DC 20056
(800) 763-9131
www.teachingforchange.org
e-mail: info@teachingforchange.org
Formerly NECA (Network of Educators on the Americas), the goal of Teaching for Change is to build social justice by introducing relevant ideas through the

schools and in the classroom. The group is affiliated with the National Coalition of Education Activists and the National Association of Multicultural Education. It is a non-profit organization that is a source for books, videos, featured resources, and posters promoting social and economic justice. One notable publication is *Teaching for Change Review.*

The Civic Mind™

(406) 582-8828

www.civicmind.org

e-mail: TheCivicMind@aol.com

Founder and lawyer-turned-activist Wendy Bay Lewis describes the purpose of The Civic Mind™ as to help others become "more effective citizen[s] by understanding civic participation and leadership." This web site includes awards bestowed on outstanding activist groups; resource directories organized by state and topic; a directory of relevant legal cases; keynote speeches Ms. Lewis has made to a wide variey of audiences on participation, education, and civic leadership; posts on "hot public issues"; and, other relevant resources including a booklist of works of interest to activists. The site offers a particularly good overview of resources for educators.

United for a Fair Economy

37 Temple Place, 2nd Floor

Boston, MA 02111

(617) 423-2148

www.stw.org

e-mail: info@faireconomy.org

Founded with the vision of building an economic movement to contest current United States economic policies and working toward closing the economic divide, UFE is a non-profit, nonpartisan organization. United for a Fair Economy provides "movement support" by supplying economic literacy education, training resources, creative tactics to support economic justice initiatives, and media capabilities. *The Nation* journalist John Nichols described UFE as "the single most effective group in the country when it comes to publicizing issues of economic injustice, income disparity, the racial underpinnings of the gap between rich and poor, and . . . the yawning chasm between the salaries of corporate CEOs and those of working Americans."

WebActive

RealNetworks, Inc.

2601 Elliott Avenue

Seattle, WA 98121

(206) 674-2240
www.webactive.com
e-mail: realimpact@real.com
Via the makers of RealAudio, RealNetworks, Inc. initiated WebActive which provides streaming media focused on progressive social activism. It is the exclusive source of Hightower Radio's commentaries on current issues. Some other features of WebActive include RadioNation, the weekly broadcasted edition of *The Nation* magazine; CounterSpin, produced by media critics Fairness and Accuracy in Reporting; Pacifica Network News, reporting world news not covered by mainstream media; and an annotated searchable directory of over 1,200 progressive organizations.

Working for Change
(877) 255-9253
www.workingforchange.com
The for-profit organization WorkingAssets claims that building business and building a better world are both possible. Published by Working Assets, this online journal *Working for Change* contains progressive news and opinion pieces by well-known journalists and authors such as Molly Ivins, Greg Palast, and Robert Scheer. Other web site features include a forum on urgent issues, a daily radio program (access www.workingassetsradio.com to listen online), and shopping at stores which donate 5% of their profits (over $35 million) to non-profits working for peace, human rights, education, ecology, and equality.

World Resources Institute
10. G Street, NE (Suite 800)
Washington, DC 20002
(202) 729-7600
about.wri.org
e-mail: front@wri.org
World Resources Institute (WRI) connects natural resource use and conservation, economic development, and social equity by promoting research, capability building, and organizational change. Focused primarily on research and policy analysis, the group's main objectives are to protect the Earth's living systems, increase information access, reverse global warming, and develop sustainable enterprise and opportunity. WRI's web site includes publications, news, Earth Trends, and Global Topics

Worldviews
(726) 298-2528
worldviews.igc.org
e-mail: worldviews@igc.org

WorldViews publicizes print and audiovisual resources produced by writers, editors, filmmakers, and others who deal with topics of peace and justice in world affairs. Particularly concerned with Latin America/the Caribbean, Asia/Pacific, Africa, and the Middle East, WorldViews offers a resource center, document search and delivery, publications, and electronic information services.

Znet

www.zmag.org

e-mail: sysop@zmag.org

The Znet community is committed to social change. The web magazine consists of feature articles, interviews, and pieces about labor, world events, economics, media and war. Video and audio links are provided as well as debates and interactive features. Another component of the site is an exchange agreement with international periodicals such as *Le Monde diplomatique* and the *New Left Review*. This resource presents a large and timely assortment of information on issues concerning social change activists.

Bibliography

Agbenyega, S., & Jiggetts, J. (1999). Minority children and their over-representation in special education [Electronic version]. *Education, 119*(4), 619–632.

Albers, P. (2002). Praxis II and African-American teacher candidates (or, is everything black bad?) [Electronic version]. *English Education, 34*(2), 105.

Albrecht, S., & Joles, C. (2003). Accountability and access to opportunity: Mutually exclusive tenets under a high stakes testing mandate [Electronic version]. *Preventing School Failure, 47*(2), 86–91.

Altwerger, B., Strauss, S. L., Labbo, L. D., & Bomer, R. (2002). The business behind testing [Electronic version]. *Language Arts, 79*(3), 256–263.

American Association of Colleges for Teacher Education. (1994). Teacher education pipeline III: Schools, colleges and departments of education enrollments by race and ethnicity. Washington, DC: Author.

American Association of Colleges for Teacher Education. (1999). Teacher education pipeline IV: Schools, colleges and departments of education enrollments by race and ethnicity. Washington, DC: Author.

American Association of University Women. (Producer). (1991). *Shortchanging girls, shortchanging America* [1 videocassette (18 min., 58 sec.)]. (Available from American Association of University Women, 1111 Sixteenth St. N.W., Washington, DC 20036).

American Civil Liberties Union. *Student Rights*. Retrieved September 29, 2003, from http://www.aclu.org/StudentsRights/StudentsRights Main.cfm.

Applebaum, M. (2003). Don't spare the brand [Electronic version]. *Brandweek, 44*(10), 20–26.

Appleman, D., & Thompson, M. (2002). "Fighting the toxic status quo": Alfie Kohn on standardized tests and teacher education. *English Education, 34*(2), 95–103.

Archer, J. (1996, August 7). Conn. Supreme Court orders desegregation for Hartford [Electronic version]. *Education Week*, 6.

Atcheson, R. (2002, January 30). *Prepping for college* [Electronic version]. Princeton Alumni Weekly. Retrieved September 30, 2003, from http://www.princeton.edu/~paw/web_exclusives/features/features_013002b.html.

Banks, J. A. (1994). *An introduction to multicultural education*. Needham Heights, MA: Allyn & Bacon.

Berkow, I. (2001, Jul 28). A deadly toll is haunting football [Electronic version]. *New York Times,* p. D1.

Berliner, D. C., & Biddle, B. J. (1996). In defense of schools [Electronic version]. *Vocational Education Journal, 71*(3), 36+.

Berliner, D. C., & Biddle, B. J. (1997). *The manufactured crisis: Myths, fraud, and the attack on America's public schools.* White Plains, NY: Longman.

Berliner, D. C. (2001, January 28.). Editorial. [Electronic version]. *The Washington Post,* p. B3.

Biddle, B. (1997). Foolishness, dangerous nonsense, and real correlates of state differences in achievement [Electronic version]. *Phi Delta Kappan, 79*(1), 8–13.

Biklen, S. K. (1995). *School work: Gender and the cultural construction of teaching.* New York: Teachers College Press.

Blair, J. (2003, May 7). Education groups seek more federal funds for high schools [Electronic version]. *Education Week,* 11.

Bowles, S., & Gintis, H. (1976). *Schooling in capitalist America: Educational reform and the contradictions of economic life.* New York: Basic Books.

Boyles, D. R. (2002). Commercialism, epistemology, and Channel One: The problem of consumer materialism, reliabilism, and an age of technophilia [Electronic version]. *Philosophical Studies in Education, 33,* 115–126.

Buchen, I. (1999). Business sees profits in education: Challenging public schools [Electronic version]. *The Futurist, 33*(5), 38–44.

Bullough, R. (2001). *Uncertain lives: Children of promise, teachers of hope.* New York: Teachers College Press.

Bush, G. H. (1990, January 31). *State of the Union Address,* retrieved September 22, 2003, from http://www.thisnation.com/library/sotu/1990gb.html.

Bush, G. W. (2001). *Foreword: No Child Left Behind Proposal* [Electronic version]. Retrieved September 12, 2003 from http://www.whitehouse.gov/news/reports/no-child-left-behind.html.

Bush, G. W. (2002). *State of the Union Address.* Retrieved September 22, 2003, from http://more.abcnews.go.com/sections/politics/dailynews/sotu_transcript020129.html.

The Business Roundtable. (2003, July 11). Retrieved July 11, 2003, from http://www.brtable.org/index.cfm.

Carr, D. (1997). Collegial leaders: Teachers who want more than just a job [Electronic version]. *The Clearing House, 70*(5), 240–243.

Center for Democracy and Citizenship. Retrieved October 12, 2003, from http://www.campaign youngvoters.org/about/center/.

Child Poverty by Race and Ethnicity: 1998 (2000). [Electronic version]. *Education Week,* 41.

Chin, M., & Newman, K. (2002). *High stakes: Time poverty, testing and the children of the working poor* (Working paper). New York: Foundation for Child Development.

Chomsky, N. (1999). *Profit over people: Neoliberalism and global order.* New York: Seven Stories Press.

Christensen, L. (2000). *Reading, writing, and rising up: Teaching about social justice and the power of the written word.* Milwaukee, WI: Rethinking Schools, Ltd.

Civil Rights Project. (2002). *Racial inequity in special education: Executive summary for federal policy makers* [Electronic version]. (Research report). Cambridge, MA: Harvard University.

Clinton, W. (1994). *State of the union message.* Retrieved September 22, 2003, from http://abcnews.go.com/sections/us/DailyNews/SOUgrid_990118.html

Cochran-Smith, M. (2000). Blind vision: Unlearning racism in teacher education. *Harvard Educational Review, 70*(2), 157.

Cohen, Y. A. (1971). The shaping of men's minds: Adaptions to the imperatives of culture. In M. L. Wax, S. Diamond, & F. O. Gearing (Eds.), *Anthropoligical perspectives on culture* (19–50). New York: Basic Books.

Coles, G. (2000). *Misreading reading: The bad science that hurts children.* Portsmouth, NH: Heinemann.

Coles, G. (2003). *Reading the naked truth: Literacy, legislation, and lies.* Portsmouth, NH: Heinemann.

Coles, G. (2003). Learning to read and the 'W Principle'. *Rethinking Schools Online, 17.* Retrieved September 12, 2003, from http://www.rethinkingschools.org/.

Consumers Union. (1990). *Captive kids: A report on commercial pressures on kids at school.* Retrieved October 10, 2003, from http://www.consumersunion.org/other/captivekids/.

Cox, S. (2003, March 4). Richmond, VA. Doing business with schools [Electronic version]. *Times Dispatch,* p.B1.

Cuban, L. (1993). *How teachers taught: Constancy and change in American classrooms, 1890–1990* (2nd ed.). New York: Teachers College Press.

Cummins, J. (2001). Empowering minority students: A framework for introduction [Electronic version]. *Harvard Educational Review, 71*(4), 649–657.

Cunningham, W. G. (2003). Grassroots democracy: Putting the public back into public education [Electronic version]. *Phi Delta Kappan, 84*(10), 776.

Cushner, K., McClelland, A., & Safford, P. L. (2000). *Human diversity in education: an integrative approach* (3rd ed.). Boston: McGraw-Hill.

Daly, J. K., Schall, P. L., & Skeele, R. W. (Eds.). (2001). *Protecting the right to teach and learn: Power, politics and public schools.* New York: Teachers College Press.

Darling-Hammond, L. (2002). What's at stake in high stakes testing? [Electronic version]. *Brown University Child and Adolescent Behavioral Letter, 18*(1), 1, 3–4.

Davis, M. R. (2002, December 11). Agency advice on new racial choices lags [Electronic version]. *Education Week,* 20, 23.

Delisio, E. (2001). *Native American schools ponder, assail dropout rates.* Retrieved June 9, 2002, from http://www.education-world.com/a_issues/issues190.shtml.

Dell-Angela, T. (2000, April 19). Gay educators discovering strength in honesty: Equal working rights don't always extend to the classroom a recent survey found [Electronic version]. *Chicago Tribune,* p. 1.1.

Delpit, L. D. (1995). *Other people's children: Cultural conflict in the classroom.* New York: New Press.

Dewey, J. (1914). *Democracy and education* (1966 ed.). New York: Free Press.

Dewey, J. (1927). *The public and its problems* (1998 ed.). Athens, Ohio: Swallow Press.

Dewey, J. (1938). *Experience and education* (1963 ed.). New York: Macmillan.

Doud, J. L., & Keller, E. P. (1998). Elementary/middle-school principals: 1998 and beyond [Electronic version]. *The Education Digest, 64*(3).

Dworkin, A. (1987). *Teacher burnout in the public schools.* Albany: State University of New York Press.

Ehrenreich, B. (2001). *Nickel and dimed: On (not) getting by in boom-time America.* New York: Metropolitan Books.

Eichelberger, J. (2002, February 21). Reading programs. Speech presented at The Secretary's Reading Leadership Academy. Washington, D.C.

Engeln, J. T. (2003). Guiding school/business partnerships [Electronic version]. *The Education Digest, 68*(7), 36–40.

Entwisle, D. R., & Alexander, K. L. (1995). A parents' economic shadow: Family structure versus family resources as influences on early school achievement [Electronic version]. *Journal of Marriage and Family, 57,* 399–409.

Evidence for homosexuality gene. (1993). *Science, 261*(5119), 291.

Fair Test. (1996). ETS creates for-profit spin-off [Electronic version]. *Fair Test Examiner.* Retrieved October 12, 2003 from http://www.fairtest.org/examarts/spring96/forprofi.htm.

Ferguson, S. (1994). The comfort of being sad. *Usne Reader,* 64, 60–61.

Fine, M., & Weis, L. (2003). *Silenced voices and extraordinary conversations: Re-imagining schools.* New York: Teachers College Press.

Fischman, G. (2000). Expanding democratic choices: Schooling for democracy—Toward a critical utopianism [Electronic version]. *Contemporary Sociology, 29*(1), 168–180.

Fox, D. (2000, August 4). Corporate-sponsored tests aim to standardize our kids: New democracy. Retrieved August 14, 2003 from http://www.newdemocracyworld.org/fox.htm.

Frankenberg, E., & Lee, C. (2002). *Race in American public schools: Rapidly re-segregating school districts* [Electronic version]. (Research report). Cambridge, MA: Harvard University.

Freire, P. (1970). *Pedagogy of the oppressed* (1987 ed.). New York: Continuum.

Freire, P. (1998). *Pedagogy of freedom: Ethics, democracy and civic courage.* Lanham, MD: Rowman and Littlefield.

Fuller, B. (2003). Federalism on the cheap [Electronic version]. *Education Week, 22*(18), 44, 30, 31.

Furr, D. (2001, October 31). Leave No Child Behind? [Electronic version]. *Education Week,* 34, 36.

Gaines, D. (1990). *Teenage wasteland: Suburbia's dead end kids.* New York: Harper Perennial.

George, P. (2002). Barriers to access and success [Electronic version]. *Principal Leadership, 2*(9), 23–29.

Giroux, H. (1988). *Teachers as intellectuals: Toward a critical pedagogy of learning.* New York: Bergin & Garvey.

Giroux, H. A. (1993). *Living dangerously: Multiculturalism and the politics of difference.* New York: Peter Lang.

Giroux, H. A. (1998). Education incorporated? [Electronic version]. *Educational Leadership, 56*(2), 12–17.

Goodlad, J. (2002). Kudzu, rabbits, and school reform [Electronic version]. *Phi Delta Kappan, 84*(1), 16.

Gratz, D. B. (2003, June 11). Leaving no child behind [Electronic version]. *Education Week,* 36, 27.

Graves, D. (2002). *Testing is not teaching: What should count in education.* Portsmouth, NH: Heinemann.

Groulx, J. G. (2001). Changing pre-service teacher perceptions of minority schools [Electronic version]. *Urban Education, 36*(1), 60.

Growing Up in Poverty Project. (2000). *Remember the children: Mothers balance work and child care under welfare reform* [Electronic version]. (Research report). University of California, Berkeley and Yale University.

Grumet, M. R. (1988). *Bitter milk: Women and teaching.* Amherst: University of Massachusetts Press.

Haberman, A. (1994). Preparing teachers for the real world of urban schools [Electronic version]. *Educational Forum, 58*(2), 162–168.

Heath, S. B. (1983). *Ways with words: Language, life, and work in communities and classrooms.* New York: Cambridge University Press.

Hendrie, C. (1998, June 10). Buffalo seeks a smooth transition after release from court oversight [Electronic version]. *Education Week,* 10.

Herszenhorn, D. (2003, July 17). City plans to add 6 standardized tests in math and English, *The New York Times,* p. B5.

Hilliard, A. G. (1984). From hurdles to standards of quality in teacher testing. *Journal of Negro Education, 55*(3), 304–315.

Hinchey, P. (1992). *Using the practical problems novice teachers articulate as routes to the theoretical thinking they dread* (Unpublished doctoral dissertation, Columbia University Teachers College, New York, 1992).

Hinchey, P. (1998). *Finding freedom in the classroom: A practical introduction to critical theory*. New York: Peter Lang Publishing.

Hinchey, P. (2001a). Learning to read the world: Who—and what—is missing? *Reading Online, 4*(10). Retrieved October 1, 2003 from http://www.readingonline.org/newliteracies/lit_index.asp?HREF=/newliteracies/hinchey/index.html.

Hinchey, P. (2001b). *Student rights*. Santa Barbara, CA: ABC-CLIO.

Hine, D., & Thompson, K. (1998). *A shining thread of hope: The history of Black women in America*. New York: Broadway Books.

Hochschild, J. (2001). Public schools and the American dream [Electronic version]. *Dissent, 48*(4), 35–42.

Hoff, D. (2003, June 4). San Francisco assignment rules anger parents [Electronic version]. *Education Week,* 9.

Hood, S., & Parker, L. J. (1994). Minority students informing the faculty: Implications for racial diversity and the future of teacher education [Electronic version]. *Journal of Teacher Education, 45,* 164–171.

hooks, b. (2000). *Where we stand: Class matters*. New York: Routledge.

Howard, G. R. (1999). *We can't teach what we don't know: White teachers, multiracial schools*. New York: Teachers College Press.

Hubler, S., & Silverstein, S. (1993, Jan 10). Schooling doesn't close minority earning gap salaries [Electronic version]. *The Los Angeles Times,* p. 1.

Hunter, P. C. (2002, February 22). Accountability. Speech presented at The Secretary's Reading Leadership Academy. Washington, DC.

Johnston, R., & Viadero, D. (2000). Unmet promise: Rising minority achievement [Electronic version]. *Education Week,* 1, 18–19.

Kao, G. (1999). Psychological well-being and educational achievement among immigrant youth. In D. J. Hernandez (Ed.), *Children of immigrants: Health, adjustment and public assistance*. Washington, DC: National Academy Press.

Katz, A. (1999). Keepin' it real: Personalizing school experiences for diverse learners to create harmony and minimize interethnic conflict, *The Journal of Negro Education, 68,* 496.

Keller, B. (1999, November 10). Women superintendents: Few and far between [Electronic version]. *Education Week,* 1.

Keller, B. (2003, January 22). Leaders in business and education take up improvement of teaching [Electronic version]. *Education Week,* 6.

Kelly, D. (1993, Jul 6). Fernandez proud of his legacy to NYC schools [Electronic version]. *USA Today,* p. 06D.

Kemple, J. J., Murnane, R. J., Singer, J. D., & Willett, J. B. (1995). Why are there fewer and fewer black teachers? In G. E. Thomas (Ed.), *Race and ethnicity in America: Meeting the challenges in the 21st century,* 91–111. Washington, DC: Taylor and Francis.

Keresty, B., O'Leary, S., & Wortley, D. (1998). *You can make a difference: A teacher's guide to political action*. Portsmouth, NH: Heinemann.

The Killing Zone (2002, Feb 23). [Electronic version]. *The Guardian,* Manchester (UK), p. 26.

Kincheloe, J. L., Slattery, P., & Steinberg, S. R. (2000). *Contextualizing teaching*. New York: Addison Wesley Longman.

Klassen, T. R., & Carr, P. D. (1997). Different perceptions of race in education: Racial minority and White teachers [Electronic version]. *Canadian Journal of Education, 22,* 67–81.

Kohn, A. (1999). Forward . . . into the past. *Rethinking Schools Online, 14*(1). Retrieved October 1, 2003 from http://www.rethinkingschools.org/.

Kozol, J. (1991). *Savage Inequalities*. New York: Crown.

Kozol, J., Wells, A., Delpit, L., Rose, M., Fruchter, N., Kohl, K., et al. (1997). Saving public education [Electronic version]. *The Nation, 264*(6), 16–25.

Kozol, J. (2002). Malign neglect [Electronic version]. *The Nation, 274* (22), 20–23.

Ladson-Billings, G. (1994). *The dreamkeepers: Successful teachers of African-American children.* San Francisco: Jossey-Bass.

Ladson-Billings, G. (2001). *Crossing over to Canaan: The journey of new teachers in diverse classrooms.* San Francisco: Jossey-Bass.

Latham, A. S., Gitomer, D., & Ziomek, R. (1999). What the tests tell us about new teachers. *Educational Leadership, 56*(8), 23–26.

Lewin, T., & Medina, J. (2003, July 31). To cut failure rate, schools shed students [Electronic version]. *The New York Times,* p. A1.

Mathis, W. J. (2003). No Child Left Behind: Costs and benefits [Electronic version]. *Phi Delta Kappan Online.* Retrieved October 1, 2003 from http://www.pdkintl.org/kappan/k0305mat.htm.

McIntosh, P. (1990). White privilege: Unpacking the invisible knapsack [Electronic version]. *Independent School, 49,* 31+.

McLanahan, S. S., & Sandefur, G. (1994). *Growing up with a single parent: What hurts, what helps?* Cambridge, MA: Harvard University Press.

Mencimer, S. (2002). Children left behind [Electronic version]. *The American Prospect, 13*(23), 29–31.

Meyer, R. (2003). Captives of the script: Killing us softly with phonics. *Rethinking Schools Online, 17*(4). Retrieved September 12, 2003 from http://www.rethinkingschools.org/.

Miner, B. (2002). Business goes to school: The for-profit corporate drive to run public schools [Electronic version]. *Multinational Monitor, 23*(1/2), 13–16.

Mueller, C., Finley, A., Iverson, R., & Price, J. (1999). The effects of group racial composition on job satisfaction, organizational commitment, and career commitment: The case of teachers [Electronic version]. *Work and Occupations, 26*(2), 187–219.

Nabokov, P. (Ed.). (1991). *Native American testimony: A chronicle of Indian-White relations from prophecy to the present, 1492–1992.* New York: Penguin.

National Commission on Excellence in Education. (1983). *A nation at risk: The imperative for educational reform* [Electronic version]. Washington, DC: U.S. Department of Education.

Ogbu, J. (1990). Minority education in comparative perspective [Electronic version]. *Journal of Negro Education, 59*(1), 45–57.

Ohanian, S. (2002). Is satire possible? [Electronic version]. *Phi Delta Kappan, 84*(4), 312–316.

Olson, L. (2000a, September 27). High Poverty Among Young Makes Schools' Job Harder [Electronic version]. *Education Week, 40,* 41.

Olson, L. (2000b, September 27). Minority Groups to Emerge as a Majority in U.S. Schools [Electronic version]. *Education Week, 34,* 35.

Olson, L. (2000c, September 27). Mixed needs of immigrants pose challenges for schools [Electronic version]. *Education Week, 38,* 39.

Olson, L. (2003a, January 8). Law's lofty goals valuable, business leaders say [Electronic version]. *Education Week,* 20.

Olson, L. (2003b, May 14). States debate exam policies for diplomas [Electronic version]. *Education Week,* 1, 22.

Orenstein, P., & American Association of University Women. (1994). *Schoolgirls: Young women, self-esteem, and the confidence gap* (1st ed.). New York: Doubleday.

Otterbourg, S. (1999). Prepping the next generation [Electronic version]. *Across the Board, 36*(2), 55.

Pailliotet, A. W. (1997). "I'm really quiet": A case study of an Asian, language minority pre-service teacher's experiences [Electronic version]. *Teaching and Teacher Education, 13*(7), 675–690.

Pallas, A., Natriello, G., & McDill, E. (1989). The changing nature of the disadvantaged population: Current dimensions and future trends [Electronic version]. *Educational Researcher, 18,* 16–22.

Palmer, P. J. (1997). The heart of a teacher [Electronic version]. *Change, 29*(6), 14–22.

Parker, W. (Ed.). (2002). *Education for democracy: Contexts, curricula, assessments.* Greenwich, CT: Information Age Publishing.

Pellicer, L. O., & Anderson, L. W. (1995). *A handbook for teacher leaders.* Thousand Oaks, CA: Corwin Press.

Perreault, G. (2000). The classroom impact of high-stress testing [Electronic version]. *Education, 120*(4), 705–710.

Perry, T., & Delpit, L. (1998). *The real ebonics debate: Power, language and the education of African-American children.* Boston: Beacon Press.

Policy Analysis for California Education. (2001, Spring). Cracks in California's Child-Care System [Electronic version]. *PACE Newsletter,* 1, 5.

Pound, E., & Stout, H. (1991, March 5). Bush nominee Alexander's investment successes have made Senate investigators very inquisitive [Electronic version]. *Wall Street Journal,* p. A18.

Price, J. (1999). Schooling and racialized masculinities: The diploma, teacher, and peers on the lives of young, African-American men [Electronic version]. *Youth And Society, 31*(2), 224–263.

Purpel, D. (2001). *Moral outrage in education.* New York: Peter Lang Publishing.

Quiocho, A., & Rios, F. (2000). The power of their presence: Minority group teachers and schooling [Electronic version]. *Review of Educational Research, 70*(4), 485–528.

Rana, J. (1998, October). Justice, Do It. *Kids Can Make A Difference Newsletter.* Retrieved August 4, 2003 from http://www.kidscanmakeadifference.org/Newsletter/n1098c.htm.

Reaching the top: A report of the national task force on minority high achievement (1999). [Electronic version]. New York: College Board Publications.

Reid, K. S. (2001, March 21). U.S. Census Underscores Diversity [Electronic version]. *Education Week,* 1, 18, 19.

Richard, A. (2002, September 4). Poor districts seen to face "funding gaps" in many states [Electronic version]. *Education Week,* 28.

Rist, R. C. (2002). HER classic: Student social class and teacher expectations: The self-fulfilling prophecy in ghetto education [Electronic version]. *Harvard Educational Review, 70*(3), 257–301.

Robelen, E. (2000, October 11). Political ads turn spotlight on education issues [Electronic version]. *Education Week,* 1, 32–33.

Robelen, E. (2001, December 31). House overwhelmingly passes sweeping reform bill. Retrieved July 11, 2003 from: http://www.edweek.com/ew/ewstory.cfm?slug=15esea_web2.h21& keywords=Robelen%20and%20reform%20bill

Robelen, E. (2003). Itemizing the budget [Electronic version]. *Education Week,* 1, 32, 33.

Robinson, J. (February 21, 2002). Reading programs. Speech presented at The Secretary's Reading Leadership Academy. Washington, DC.

Rofes, E. (2000). Young adult reflections on having an openly gay teacher during early adolescence [Electronic version]. *Education and Urban Society, 32*(3), 399.

Rothstein, R. (1993). The myth of public school failure [Electronic version]. *The American Prospect, 4*(13), 20–34.

Roulston, K., & Mills, M. (2000). Male teachers in feminised teaching areas: Marching to the beat of the men's movement drums? [Electronic version]. *Oxford Review of Education, 26*(2), 221–238.

Rumberger, R. W., & Larson, K. A. (1998). The changing nature of the disadvantaged population: Current dimensions and future trends [Electronic version]. *Educational Researcher, 18,* 16–22.

Sadker, M., & Sadker, D. M. (1994). *Failing at fairness : How America's schools cheat girls.* New York: Charles Scribner's Sons.

Saltman, K. J. (2000). *Collateral damage: Corporatizing public schools—A threat to democracy.* New York: Rowman & Littlefield.

Schabner, D. (2003). *Blood for Books: Some parents are tapping a vein for kids' schools—Is anything enough?* Retrieved August 11, 2003 from http://abcnews.go.com/sections/us/WorldNews Tonight/schoolbud getso30514.html.

Schaeffer, B. (1996). *Standardized tests and teacher competence.* Retrieved June 9, 2003, from http://www.fairtest.org/empl/tt comp.htm

Seltzer, R., Frazier, M., & Ricks, I. (1995). Multiculturalism, race and education [Electronic version]. *Journal of Negro Education, 64*(2), 124–140.

Shannon, P. (1992). *Becoming political: Readings and writings in the politics of literacy education.* Portsmouth, NH: Heinemann.

Shepard, L. (Winter, 2002/2003). The hazards of high-stakes testing [Electronic version]. *Issues in Science and Technology, 19*(2), 53–58.

Shor, I., & Freire, P. (1987). *A pedagogy for liberation: Dialogues on transforming education.* South Hadley, MA: Bergin & Garvey.

Shor, I. (1992). *Empowering education: Critical teaching for social change.* Chicago: University of Chicago Press.

Shor, I., & Pari, C. (1999). *Education is politics: Critical teaching across differences, K-12.* Portsmouth, NH: Boynton/Cook.

Singham, M. (1998). The canary in the mine [Electronic version]. *Phi Delta Kappan, 80*(1), 8–15.

Sizer, T. R. (1985). *Horace's compromise: The dilemma of the American high school.* Boston: Houghton Mifflin.

Solmitz, D. O. (2001). *Schooling for humanity: When big brother isn't watching.* New York: Peter Lang.

Spring, J. (1988). *Conflict of interests: The politics of American education.* New York: Longman.

Spring, J. (1994). *Deculturalization and the struggle of equality.* New York: McGraw-Hill.

Spring, J. (1996). *American education* (7th ed.). New York: McGraw-Hill.

Spring, J. (1997). *The American school 1642-1996* (4th ed.). New York: McGraw-Hill.

Spritzler, J. (1998). *Corporations meet resistance inside Boston's schools.* New Democracy. Retrieved June 4, 2003 from http://www.newdemocracyworld.org/schools.htm

Stevens, L. P. (April 2003). Reading first: A critical policy analysis [Electronic version]. *The Reading Teacher, 56*(7), 662–669.

Stratman, D. (1997). *School reform and the attack on public education* [Electronic version]. (Keynote Address to the Massachusetts Association of School Superintendents Summer Institute).

Strauss, S. L. (2002). Politics and reading at the National Institute of Child Health and Human Development [Electronic version]. *Pediatrics, 109*(1), 143–144.

Strauss, V. (2000, December 26). When success doesn't add up: How can a "Nation at Risk" continue to thrive when U.S. students score so poorly on math and science tests? [Electronic version]. *The Washington Post,* p. A 12.

Strauss, V. (2002a, Mar 19, 2002). An assignment to rethink the idea of homework; More parents are questioning whether there aren't better ways to help in their kids' education [Electronic version]. *The Los Angeles Times,* p. E2.

Strauss, V. (2002b, September 10). Phonics pitch irks teachers; U.S. denies it's pushing commercial products [Electronic version]. *The Washington Post,* p. A.01.

Su, Z. (1997). Teaching as a profession and as a career: Minority candidates' perspectives [Electronic version]. *Teaching and Teacher Education, 13,* 325–340.

Sulentic, M. (2001). Black English in a place called Waterloo [Electronic version]. *Multicultural Education, 8*(4), 24–30.

Sumsion, J. (2000). Rewards, risks and tensions: Perceptions of males enrolled in an early childhood teacher education programme [Electronic version]. *Asia-Pacific Journal of Teacher Education, 28*(1), 87–101.

Tamboukou, M. (2000). The paradox of being a woman teacher [Electronic version]. *Gender and Education, 12*(4), 463–478.

Tate, W. (1994). Race, retrenchment, and the reform of school mathematics [Electronic version]. *Phi Delta Kappan, 76,* 477–484.

Tatum, B. D. (1997). *"Why are all the Black kids sitting together in the cafeteria?"* New York: Basic Books.

Terrill, M. M., & Mark, D. L. H. (2000). Pre-service teachers' expectations for schools with children of color and second-language learners [Electronic version]. *Journal of Teacher Education, 51*(2), 149.

Thomas, S. M. P. (1999). Everything I need to know about edbusfotainment, I learned from my kid [Electronic version]. *The Journal for Quality and Participation, 22*(2), 41–43.

Thrupkaew, N. (June 3, 2002). A dollar short [Electronic version]. *The American Prospect,* 13–14.

Titus, J. (2000). Engaging student resistance to feminism: "How is this stuff going to make us better teachers?" [Electronic version]. *Gender and Education, 12*(1), 21–37.

Toch, T. (1998). The curse of low expectations [Electronic version]. *U.S. News & World Report, 125*(13), 60+.

Trends in the well-being of America's children & youth 2001. (2001). Washington, DC: Department of Health and Human Services.

Tyack, D. B. (1974). *The one best system : A history of American urban education.* Cambridge, Mass.: Harvard University Press.

Untitled. (2001, January 23). *Business Wire.*

U. S. Bureau of Census. (2002). *Public elementary and secondary school teachers—Selected characteristics: 1993–94* (No. 236). Washington, D.C.: Congressional Information Service.

Walsh, M. (1998, January 1). Teacher fights gag order [Electronic version]. *Education Week,* 34–39.

Walsh, M. (2002, October 30). High court declines case on harassment of gay teacher [Electronic version]. *Education Week,* 28.

Weiss, D. (2002). Confronting White privilege. *Rethinking Schools Online, 16*(4). Retrieved October 1, 2003 from http://www.rethinking schools.org

Welsh, P. (2003, June 15). Passing scores fail my students [Electronic version]. *The Washington Post,* p. B 03.

West, C. (1993). *Race matters.* Boston: Beacon Press.

Wilder, M. (2000). Increasing African-American teachers' presence in American schools: Voices of students who care [Electronic version]. *Urban Education, 35*(2), 2–5–220.

Wilensky, R. (2001, May 9). Wrong, wrong, wrong [Electronic version]. *Education Week,* 48, 32.

Willie, C. V. (2000). Confidence, trust and respect: The preeminent goals of educational reform [Electronic version]. *The Journal of Negro Education, 69*(4), 255–263.

Willis, A., & Lewis, K. (1999). Our known everydayness: Beyond a response to white privilege [Electronic version]. *Urban Education, 34*(2), 245–262.

Wink, J. (2000). *Critical pedagogy: Notes from the real world* (2nd ed.). New York: Longman.

Wise, T. (2002). Membership has its privileges. *Rethinking Schools Online 16*(4). Retrieved October 10, 2003 from http:// www. rethinkingschools.org

Wolffe, R. (1996). Reducing pre-service teachers' negative expectations of urban field experience [Electronic version]. *Teacher Education Quarterly, 23*(1), 99–106.

Wright, R. G. (1997). *Selling words: Free speech in a commercial culture.* New York: New York University Press.

Zeichner, K. (1996). Educating teachers for cultural diversity. In K. Zeichner, S. Meinich, & M. Gomez (Eds.), *Currents of reform in pre-service teacher education.* New York: Teachers College Press.

Zill, N., Collins, N., West, J., & Germino-Hauskeen, E. (1995). *Approaching kindergarten: A look at preschoolers in the United States, NCES 95–280.* Washington, D.C.: U.S. Department of Education.

Zill, N. (1996). Family change and student achievement: What we have learned, what it means for schools. In A. Booth & J. P. Dunn (Eds.), *Family-school links: How do they affect educational outcomes?* Hillside, NJ: Lawrence Erlbaum Associates.

Zill, N., & West, J. (2000). Entering kindergarten: A portrait of American children when they begin school. In *The Condition of Education 2000, NCES 2000–062.* Washington, DC: U.S. Department of Education.

Zimpher, N. (1989). The RATE project: A profile of teacher education students [Electronic version]. *Journal of Teacher Education, 40*(3), 27–30.

Index

Studies in the Postmodern Theory of Education

General Editors
Joe L. Kincheloe & Shirley R. Steinberg

Counterpoints publishes the most compelling and imaginative books being written in education today. Grounded on the theoretical advances in criticalism, feminism, and postmodernism in the last two decades of the twentieth century, Counterpoints engages the meaning of these innovations in various forms of educational expression. Committed to the proposition that theoretical literature should be accessible to a variety of audiences, the series insists that its authors avoid esoteric and jargonistic languages that transform educational scholarship into an elite discourse for the initiated. Scholarly work matters only to the degree it affects consciousness and practice at multiple sites. Counterpoints' editorial policy is based on these principles and the ability of scholars to break new ground, to open new conversations, to go where educators have never gone before.

For additional information about this series or for the submission of manuscripts, please contact:

Joe L. Kincheloe & Shirley R. Steinberg
c/o Peter Lang Publishing, Inc.
275 Seventh Avenue, 28th floor
New York, New York 10001

To order other books in this series, please contact our Customer Service Department:

(800) 770-LANG (within the U.S.)
(212) 647-7706 (outside the U.S.)
(212) 647-7707 FAX

Or browse online by series:

www.peterlangusa.com